D1037554

NOTMYJESUS

OUR SACRED ROLE IN A CHANGING WORLD

BOB FABEY

All Scripture quotations, unless otherwise indicated, are taken from the Holy Bible, New International Version®, NIV®. Copyright ©1973, 1978, 1984, 2011 by Biblica, Inc.™ Used by permission of Zondervan. All rights reserved worldwide. www.zondervan.com The "NIV" and "New International Version" are trademarks registered in the United States Patent and Trademark Office by Biblica, Inc.™

Copyright © 2018 Bob Fabey
All rights reserved.

Hardback: 978-1-64085-184-9
Paperback: 978-1-64085-183-2

Dedication

For Amy, Hannah, and J.P.

I can't imagine life and love without you.
You are beautiful, brave, and full of wonder and grace.
Thank you for loving me and teaching me
how to love.

CONTENTS

*"They would change their tune, they would
add another measure, If they only knew this
love of another kind."—Amy Grant*

INTRODUCTION

We like to make people into our own image. At the very least, we try to make ourselves like others. We will cut our hair or wear clothes like our favorite celebrity, football player, or even world leader. If you are old enough to remember, many ladies couldn't help getting their hair cut like Princess Diana. It goes in the opposite direction as well. Cultures have a way of shaping historical figures into who they want them to be. Just look around the globe at the images of St. Nicholas. In England, he is skinny. In Africa, he is black. In other places, he is a dwarf! In the United States, he is of course rotund and jovial.

Whether these have anything to do with the historic St. Nicholas isn't so much the point. The point is, each culture will view him through their particular lens. Just the mention of his name brings a thought and an image into your own mind almost immediately, I'm sure.

Jesus is no different in how He is treated by every culture. He has often been depicted as blonde-haired and blue-eyed. Or again, in Africa, He and the entire Holy Family are portrayed as black. Rarely is He ever represented as a small Jewish man who learned the art of carpentry.

Movies have done this reframing and reimaging of Jesus over and over, from the blonde-haired to the blue-eyed to the seemingly ridiculous, ninja-fighting Jesus we see in *Talladega Nights*. In this film, a NASCAR driver played by Will Ferrell is giving thanks for the family meal and doing just what we've been looking at. I think it's worth quoting the entire scene. Present at the meal are Carley, his wife, and Cal, his friend and teammate, plus Chip, his father-in-law, and his sons: Walker and Texas Ranger. The following is an excerpt of the prayer:

Ricky: Dear Lord Baby Jesus, or as our brothers to the South call you, Jesús, we thank you so much for this bountiful harvest of Domino's, KFC, and the always delicious Taco Bell. I just want to take time to say thank you for my family, my two beautiful, beautiful, handsome, striking sons, Walker and Texas Ranger, or T.R. as we call him, and of course, my red-hot smoking wife, Carley, who is a stone-cold fox. … Also, I want to thank you for my best friend and teammate, Cal Naughton Jr., who's got my back no matter what.

Cal: Shake and Bake.

Ricky: Dear Lord Baby Jesus, we also thank you for my wife's father, Chip. We hope that you can use your Baby Jesus powers to heal him and his horrible leg. And it smells terrible, and the dogs are always bothering with it. Dear tiny, infant Jesus, we—

Carley: Hey, you know, sweetie, Jesus did grow up. You don't always have to call Him "baby." It's a bit odd and off-putting to pray to a baby.

Ricky: Well, I like the Christmas Jesus best, and I'm saying grace. When you say grace, you can say it to grown-up Jesus, or teenage Jesus, or bearded Jesus, or whoever you want.

Carley: You know what I want? I want you to do this grace good so that God will let us win tomorrow.

Ricky: Dear tiny Jesus, in your golden-fleece diapers, with your tiny, little, fat, balled-up fists—

Chip: He was a man! He had a beard!

Ricky: Look, I like the baby version the best, do you hear me? I win the races, and I get the money.

Carley: Ricky, finish the damn grace.

Cal: I like to picture Jesus in a tuxedo T-shirt, 'cause it says, like, "I wanna be formal, but I'm here to party, too." Cause I like to party, so I like my Jesus to party.

Walker: I like to picture Jesus as a ninja fighting off evil samurai.

Cal: I like to think of Jesus, like, with giant eagle's wings. And singing lead vocals for Lynyrd Skynyrd, with, like, an angel band. And I'm in the front row, and I'm hammered drunk.

Carley: Hey Cal, why don't you just shut up?

Cal: Yes, ma'am.

Ricky: Okay. Dear 8-pound, 6-ounce newborn infant Jesus, don't even know a word yet, just a little infant and so cuddly, but still omnipotent, we just thank you for all the races I've won and the 21.2 million dollars—woo! (The rest of the family says "woo" too.) love that money—that I have accrued over this past season. Also, due to a binding endorsement contract that stipulates I mention Powerade at each grace, I just want to say that Powerade is delicious, and it cools you off on a hot summer day. And we look forward to Powerade's release of Mystic Mountain Blueberry. Thank you for all your power and your grace, dear Baby God. Amen.[1]

This scene is hilarious and sad at the same time. It was funny to me because of the childish way Ricky insisted upon doing things his way and how others shared how they saw Jesus. It was sad because there is a little truth to it. Many people simply see Jesus the way they want to. Somewhere on their journey, they found an image of Jesus they liked and they stuck with it. The problem with that is that people wind up looking at Jesus in part, one aspect—and maybe even a distorted one—and not the whole. When they do that, they wind up living the same way. In part. Not whole.

Growing up in Montana isn't so different from your average American childhood (although *every* Montanan would lead you to believe it was!). Schools, friends, neighbors, parents, a brother, dogs, sports, and other things were the norm for me as a kid. Church, however, was not. My first memories of worship are of making a mess opening Christmas presents at home and then sitting in St. Francis Xavier church. I looked at the stained glass and the fantastic paintings on the ceiling of the sanctuary and played with my Micronauts while wondering why everyone stood and mumbled and sat down again. There was nothing particularly spiritual or meaningful about it, just playing with my Christmas presents quietly in the pew.

This was my parents' faith, or faith as they knew it. Both had been raised in the Roman Catholic Church on the East Coast. Both had left the Church, but probably would say, if push came to shove, that they were Christians. Attending church was an obligation for them on important days, and it was something you were supposed to expose your kids to. Faith was more of an open question. Mom was practical and put one foot forward, one a day at a time. She believed, but she had lost faith in much of what she had been taught. My dad, however, was truly looking for something.

After leaving the Roman Catholic Church, Dad ventured down many paths searching for a faith that made sense in his heart. He pursued, among other things, several stages of Mormonism, and he was looking down the road of Satanism when he met Jesus. Although he knew all the stories and had a sense of the answers, Dad had never experienced a relationship with God through Jesus Christ. After meeting with a Baptist pastor who explained his deep need for a Savior, Dad trusted Jesus. What that meant was a myriad of things. It meant that he was an infant, but a Vietnam Vet. He was an infant, and yet a husband. He was an infant, but a father. Learning how to live a new life as a spiritual adult would not be easy for him or the family.

I came to "faith" in this environment. I remember that "church" one morning was watching a televange-list. I sat with my dad, watching how the man sweated profusely, raised his voice and the Bible, and talked about hell. I didn't know Jesus, so if I died, it would be without Him. According to the guy on TV, that meant I was going to hell. I imagined Yosemite Sam poking me in the butt with a pitchfork for eternity.

At six or seven years old, this was a pretty rough thought. My friends lived across the street, and we were always rushing out the door and into the street to ride bikes or play games. Not that the road was busy, but I figured it wouldn't take much for me to get whacked by a car. The preacher explained that trusting Jesus was the only way not to have an eternal date with the Warner Brothers bad guy, so I did what any kid would do—I trusted Jesus out of fear of hell. Now that I have a nimbler theology, I cringe when I see pastors use this tactic. How do they get on TV anyway? I guess fear sells.

Anyway, because my dad was a newbie and I didn't have anyone to help me understand what had happened, my picture of Jesus was woefully incomplete. I got the idea that Jesus and sin didn't go together, but I wasn't sure what the relationship was between them.

The following day, I sinned. I know—shocking, right? I don't remember what it was, exactly, or how I even knew it was a sin, but at the time I knew. It scared me because I thought that meant that Jesus wasn't with me anymore. Since He doesn't like sin, when I do it, He leaves, right?

So I asked Jesus back into my heart again. Jesus, being the good Savior that He is, unpacked His bags and took up residence in my heart again. Why does He live in my heart? That's weird, I thought. Anyway, no sooner did He put His shoes away than I sinned again. I'm pretty sure it was my brother's fault, but I bowed my head quickly to block the door from His departure and asked Him not to leave. This went on and on. I probably did it thirty times that afternoon, living in fear of Jesus taking off. At some point, I stopped doing it. Not sinning—I was good at that. I stopped asking Jesus not to leave. I guess I thought He would have to take me or leave me, sin and all.

At this time, I had an idea about Jesus that compelled me to act a certain way. My concept shaped my behavior, thoughts, and even emotions. *If you think someone is going to leave every time you make a mistake, it doesn't take long to feel like a failure, and I felt like a spiritual disappointment.*

> If you think someone is going to leave every time you make a mistake, it doesn't take long to feel like a failure, and I felt like a spiritual disappointment.

The way we view Jesus is critical. Our view affects everything. If you don't believe in Jesus, then you behave like you don't believe. If you have belief, but it is skewed, you behave and think a certain way (enter Mystic Mountain Blueberry here). I think you get my point. This happens for individuals and it plays out collectively.

People talk about "Christians" as if we are all the same. They think we all look the same. We all act the same way. We are all in the same stage of recovering our identity. We all talk the same way. (Heaven knows this isn't true! Some of us are saltier-tongued than others!) We all vote the same way. We can be counted on to behave similarly regarding given social issues. But none of those assumptions are correct. Christians are more like a mosaic—many different pieces that hopefully make a more complete representation of Jesus to the world.

Unfortunately, that isn't always the case, as we tend to fall in love with our own ideas about Him. In addressing this issue, I have collected some ways in which people like to view Jesus. They are taken from cultural observations and conversations I've had over the years. When you read them, see if you don't identify with one or more. See if you don't feel an inward calling toward healing the partial or distorted perception of Christ you hold so that you can not only represent Him more completely in the world but also live a life that is whole and immersed in a richer, deeper relationship with God.

CHAPTER 1
HE'S JUST NOT YOUR TYPE

It's funny. Your God looks a lot like you.

—Drew Collins

It's common for people to recast important figures in a light that helps them. You only have to look at your own home and family as an example. Parents often comment, "I still think of you as that cute little girl. Pigtails, snuggly and always laughing." This despite the fact that the cute little girl has grown, left home, gone to college, graduated, and started a career of her choosing. Moms, dads, brothers, and sisters often cast their loved ones in the light of what they once knew and liked. "You will always be (fill in the blank) to me."

It can be incredibly annoying when this happens to us. We grow, change, mature, and evolve. We don't look, act, or think the way we used to. But, instead of getting to know us now, many opt to stay where they were and try to relate to us that way. You can hear the exasperated 20-something yell, "I'm not a little kid anymore!"

> For some reason, we also do this with Jesus. We find a version of Him we like, and we stick with it.

For some reason, we also do this with Jesus. We find a version of Him we like, and we stick with it. Even though there are different views, we opt for the bits we like most and propagate them in our minds and in our lives.

What follows is a look at some of the ways people do this. Some are more obvious than others. You will no doubt recognize these depictions in your own life and maybe in the lives of those around you. As you do, I encourage you to hold to your view loosely. There's no telling what might happen.

The Baby/Christmas Jesus

Even people who don't follow Christianity observe Christmas. They give presents and take time off work. They talk about the "holidays" without much reference to the historicity of the event. In their minds, Christmas conjures busy schedules and perhaps even materialism. The Jesus of Christmas may mean a worship service or a recollection of worship services as a child. This Jesus remains a distant, unrelated figure, loosely connected to what is happening in their lives.

If Jesus does somehow play a role, it is as a baby. He was just the baby in a manger a long time ago. There He sits. In a manger (whatever that is), not crying—because baby Jesus didn't cry. He didn't poop or vomit

His mother's milk. He never suckled Mary's breast. He didn't have colic or diaper rashes.

He lies eerily quiet somewhere on the stage like the doll we see in so many Christmas productions. He is a placeholder with no lines. He's there, but not really. He never grew up. He isn't related to God, and He certainly isn't one who would judge the world. A silhouette of Joseph leading a donkey with a pregnant Mary on its back is the only other image of context added to this picture.

This view makes it difficult for Jesus to play a role in people's daily lives. I mean, how much of a role can a two-thousand-year-old baby play? He is the shadowy figure of a moment in history that some people think is important—but that is about it.

Medieval paintings of Him are weird. He's like a tiny adult but depicted in baby places. He's on His mom's lap, in a crib/bed-type thing but with adult appendages, or with a crown and scepter—as a baby. These paintings create a form of cognitive dissonance. When Jesus never leaves the manger, you get the idea that God is there, and for some reason, He cares about you in some way, but there isn't much past that. Many live their lives like this. Theologically, they are theists, but not Christians. Over the years, I have talked with hundreds of people like this. They understand God is there, but it doesn't really matter because He doesn't play a role in their daily lives.

The Northern European Jesus

Jesus was Jewish. He was probably short, maybe 5'5" or similar. He likely had dark hair, a dark beard, and dark eyes. Why is it, then, that many pictures of Jesus give Him blonde hair and blue eyes? His fair, pale skin makes Him look far more Nordic than Middle Eastern. Perhaps this is because artists paint people to look like themselves or their intended audience. Have you ever seen the Holy Family as depicted in Ethiopia or other parts of Africa? They aren't white.

Northern European Jesus is decidedly Western in just about every way. If He were featured on a map, Europe or North America would be at the center of that map. Of course, Jesus spoke English (because all blonde-haired, blue-eyed people do), used the King James Version of the Bible, and ate with utensils. He looked longingly and thoughtfully up to the heavens for His selfies and was always calm. His six-foot-plus frame was firm, but not too muscular. It isn't too far-fetched to think of Jesus as a Viking—just nicer.

This Jesus sits above dinner tables or on other walls in the homes of the devout. You can see Him staring into space yet providing a stern presence. Jesus is there, although it isn't altogether clear what He is doing. Is He blessing people? reminding them He's around? creating an impossible-to-live-up-to standard of holiness in His blondeness?

If you happen to be Northern European, I have bad news. He wasn't.

The Santa Claus Jesus

According to a popular Christmas song, Santa is a list-making, naughty-or-nice-judging, all-knowing fella you'd better watch out for!

Without knowing it, people think of Jesus in this Jolly Ol' Saint Nick way. It is evident by their actions. They believe if they do the right things, like going to worship and being nice, then God will do nice things for them. Jesus carries a giant ledger, and He is taking note of all the good and bad things you have done; and if your good outweighs the bad, you get rewarded. If your bad outweighs the good, you get punished with coal in your stocking—or worse, hell.

Maybe the songwriter was thinking of Jesus when he wrote about Santa. He describes an all-knowing, list-making, cry/pout-hating guy who is coming. He's coming, and if you have been bad, you are going to get it! Or not, as the case may be.

I have spoken to many Christians who think this way about Jesus. God somehow owes them something because they haven't done anything wrong. They have made such great sacrifices—good things should come, and bad things shouldn't happen to them. Plus, they are better than their neighbor, Jonny, who is an evil character. Jonny cusses, smokes, got a divorce, and cheated on his taxes. Since they don't do any of those horrible things, God owes them. They are obviously better than Jonny.

They will vigorously question God when coal arrives in the stocking—when cancer or other tragedies strike. "I'm a good person. I'm a nice guy. Why is God doing this to me?" Or even worse, when someone has been in ministry their whole lives and suddenly a loved one endures suffering, they say, "How can God allow this to happen when I have done so much for Him?"

Those are real questions, and that is real pain. When Jesus is Santa, it makes sense. But is He really? Is this the mature, healthy way of seeing your Savior?

The Nice Guy Jesus

Let's face it, most people would agree that Jesus was a "nice guy." This popular version of Jesus is viewed selectively as the one who would never be mean to anyone and only had nice things to say. Far from what we find in the Scriptures, this Jesus is the champion of a modern definition of love. This version says, "Jesus loves everyone, so whatever you want is okay."

Jesus accepted everyone! He was the champion of the least and the lost. If there were marginalized people anywhere of any stripe, He was there to protect and defend them. The woman at the well comes to mind. In John 4, a woman who is a Samaritan (more on this later) goes to a well in the middle of the day to avoid others. She meets Jesus, and despite her checkered past, He is kind to her. Or what about the woman caught in adultery? When she is dragged before Him and the rest of the town, He doesn't condemn her. Jesus is always nice. He only wants to help. He loves everyone and accepts everyone and everything.

Whenever a difficult moral situation arises, this idea of Jesus is invoked. "Jesus would never do that." "He wouldn't judge, so you shouldn't either." This Jesus is the moral high-ground for every argument or difficulty presented by today's standards. For the adherents of this Jesus, He only taught about love and acceptance and calls His followers to do the same.

With this understanding, Jesus is linked to (and, in some cases, enmeshed with) anyone who is considered a great teacher—Buddha, Gandhi, Oprah, and whoever else gets quoted on a Facebook page. Jesus melts into the ethereal backdrop as a guiding principle but not someone who would ask you to leave everything behind and follow Him, especially to the cross. Jesus is the Savior (but not the Lord).

This understanding happened by accident. In an effort to help people find faith in Jesus, Billy Graham did a fantastic job of evangelism. Beginning in the middle of the 20th century in North America and around the globe, the good news was shared. Many others followed a similar course, and sharing the gospel with loads of people at once became the norm. Similarly, organizations found ways to tell the good news in bite-sized, manageable pieces.

It wound up looking like this: "God loves you, but you are sinful. Jesus died for you, and you have to receive Him. If you do, you won't go to hell." That's it in a nutshell. Is it true? Yes. Is it complete? In no way.

I understand why Mr. Graham and others did what they did. In fact, this shrinking of the gospel may have come from elsewhere. It is a noble thing to want to reach as many people as you can for Christ. However, in my opinion, this only tells part of the good news. The gospel (a word literally meaning "good news") is that Jesus is Lord! He is the Lord over life, sin, hell, and death. He is Lord, and money, governments, corporations, the powerful, and the influential are not. That is the good news.

But many live with the idea that Jesus can be their Savior and not their Lord. This means that God loves them, Jesus died for them, and they will go to heaven because they said yes to Him. The problem is that, for them, Jesus isn't Lord. He isn't the Lord of their life. He isn't the Lord of their thoughts, pocketbooks, tongues, attitudes, or any other part of their lives. He's there to make sure they get into heaven, but He has nothing to do with their lives on earth.

Jesus saves them for a future date to be with Him, but the here and now is theirs. Unfortunately, too many Christians fit into this category. Believing in the Nice Guy Jesus is the easy route. You don't have to do anything too hard, and you can be nice to everyone around you because Jesus was nice.

I think Brennan Manning said it best: "The greatest single cause of atheism in the world today is Christians: Christians who acknowledge Jesus with their lips, walk out the door, and deny Him by their lifestyle. That is what an unbelieving world simply finds unbelievable."

The Genie Jesus

This wish-granting Jesus depends on you "rubbing" Him the right way. If you are singing "Genie in a Bottle" by Christina Aguilera right now, I have done my job! This version of Jesus is similar to the Santa Jesus. Genie Jesus will grant your wishes, however wild they may be. All you have to do is do what He wants.

His "rubbing" looks like the following: Genie Jesus wants me to be nice. If I'm nice, I get a wish. He wants me to go to church. If I go to church, I get a wish. If I don't hate anyone, or if at least I'm not as bad as so-and-so, then I get a wish! You only get a few, so make them count!

No relationship is necessary; you only have to ask. You don't need to plan for how you will follow Him or know what it means to be His or part of His people. No, He is there to make all your wildest dreams come true.

People say things like, "When I get to heaven, I'm going to bounce on the clouds, have Ferraris, money, and that pet chimpanzee I always wanted!" Jesus exists to make all your wishes come true and provide a heaven for you to live in when you die. Remember putting Northern Europe at the center of the map? Forget about that. Believing in the Genie Jesus puts *you* at the center of the map—or, more accurately, the center of the universe. Awesome!

"You ain't never had a friend like me!"

—Genie from *Aladdin*[2]

The Cosmic Cop Jesus

Maybe in part derived from the Santa Jesus, the all-knowing-cosmic-universal Cop Jesus is busy patrolling the heavens and earth looking to give out tickets to those who make mistakes. Jesus is around every corner and, in fact, lays speed traps for you when you least expect it. He is all about laws. He is the keeper of the Law (with a capital L) and all other laws, and He's just waiting for you to blow it. Making you pay brings Him joy, so, with a lightning bolt in hand, He is ready to zap those unfortunate enough to get caught breaking the divine law. The zap could be something as little as a red light when you are in a hurry or the death of a loved one. But you will pay. There is no relationship here, only punishment—but only if you get caught.

What kind of life does this lead to? Many will avoid the Cosmic Cop Jesus at all costs because they know what they have done, and they don't want Him to catch them. They live in fear, despair, or at a minimum, a lingering sense of panic brought about by the impending doom they know they'll have to face someday. This is one way to live. But, if I'm honest, simply avoiding mistakes or living in fear of doing the wrong thing is not living; it is existing, and it isn't much of an existence.

The Rendezvous Jesus

Unwittingly, we may sometimes believe we have something to offer Jesus that can, in some way, equal what He has for us. "Since I went to worship you, Jesus, you are going to give me that promotion. Right?"

This version of Jesus makes me think of the 18th- and 19th-century fur trappers in North America. At a particular time of year, these trappers would gather to drink, eat, trade, and carry on. It was called a rendezvous. (This was the French term at the time for a drunken free-for-all.) Now, when it comes to Jesus, for some it's like trading pelts for pounds of salt or bacon. We'll come together, sing a little, do some business, maybe pray, carry on for about an hour, and then head our separate ways. It is a simple exchange between supposed equals. If I give you this, then you do this. It implies we know what we need and know what is best for us.

This view of Jesus is mostly applied when we are in need. Life creates opportunities for us to call out to God, whether it's through times of sickness, job or family problems, or pain in our relationships with one another. I remember telling Jesus in a drunken stupor that if He got me home safely, I would live my life the way He wanted me to live.

Maybe you have prayed similar prayers.

"If you heal my son, then I'll give money to the church."

"Help me pass this test, and I'll be nice to my brother."

Jesus is happy to barter with us, so we offer Him what we think He wants and He will simply give us the thing we really want. The good news is He wants us to come to Him, and over time, we recognize that He doesn't always trade with us for what we want, but we get what we need.

The Divine Jesus

This image of Jesus never used the bathroom. He never passed gas. He never burped or had a bad hair day. He never had sleep in His eyes or a kink in His neck. His feet never hurt, and His back never ached. He didn't have to fight off sexual temptation because He had no genitals. Jesus was an angel. He was a different being altogether. He had wings and glowed. Around His head was a halo. Sure, He ate and slept, but that was only as an example. He didn't really have to do those things.

This version is more pervasive than you may think. When Jesus healed people or called them to follow, He merely pushed the "God button," and it worked. People slipped under His spell and followed in some trance-like obedience. When faced with temptations common to being human, He just reverted to His divine state and overcame them. When He suffered, He turned the God-stuff on so He could handle it. Why do we see Him this way? Maybe it's because we feel there is no way a human could do what He did.

It is difficult for many to think of Jesus as fully human, so they don't. He was too amazing. He was incredible; there is no way He struggled with what I struggle with. He didn't say what I say, think what I think, or do what I do. Jesus was just spirit, it seems, and He floated through our earthly dimension only to return to the fluffy, divine space called heaven. Thanks, Gnostics.

The Interplanetary Jesus

Jesus was so far from our human experience that some believe He was from another world. How else could someone heal people, dispense wisdom, walk on water and through walls, return from the dead, read minds, and help start a revolution? Television shows like *Ancient Aliens* help further this idea. He had to be an alien because we have no other category for Him.

This explains so much. Aliens are at the root of all things—creation, evolution—helping us get back on track. They are out there, watching our every move. Living outside of what we know as time-space, Jesus could cover lots of ground without effort. He could be one of many aliens. You could write an entire epic around this Jesus with backstories, origins, and love stories! The Trekkies and Star Wars fans might love it! "Make it so, Jesus." Or even "Jesus, I am your Father!"

It is easy, then, to dismiss Christianity and all other religions as having alien origins. Since He was an alien, we don't need to take Him too seriously. We can't really have a meaningful relationship with an alien. All we have to do is make crop circles and answer all difficult questions with "aliens."

Why did people make the Nazca Lines? Aliens.
Why did people make the pyramids? Aliens.
Where did the universe come from? Aliens.
Where does that one sock go from the drier? Aliens.

The Mythological Jesus

As a history major, I really enjoy discussing this particular way people view Jesus. He was just a myth. When asked, some people say He never really existed. People just made Him up. While I try to give credit to people for being reasonably intelligent, myself included, this one is hard to swallow. Some people just can't or won't believe Jesus even existed. Whenever someone or something reaches "mythical" proportions—meaning, to them, something that simply can't be true—it ceases to be real.

A slight twist on this is that Jesus did exist, but He wasn't who people made Him out to be. They look at other historical figures and point to inconsistencies or downright wrong information we have about them, and they believe the same is true for Jesus. He is merely a sociohistorical construct. As an example, Jesus was Mary and Joseph's son. They had to leave their hometown for some reason, but it wasn't because of Herod. They made up the story of her pregnancy so they wouldn't get in trouble for having a child out of wedlock. Jesus was a carpenter and learned the trade from His dad. He got lost in Jerusalem, but not for long, and was found near the temple, but not *in* it, and especially not teaching!

He was a smart boy and occasionally asked questions the teachers of the Law had trouble with, but nothing like the Bible says. He wound up having friends and some followers, but He ran afoul of Rome. He was crucified like a lot of other criminals. His friends made up the stories about His resurrection. Once they did that, they also made up stories about His teaching and healing. He became something more than a man through the centuries and evolved into the figure we see today.

This is a prevalent version of Jesus. Here and now is not the place to dissect it, but suffice it to say that there are significant problems with this theory beyond the simple fact that it is, historically, not true.

The Westboro Baptist Jesus

To give voice to as many versions of Jesus that exist, I now bring you the Westboro Baptist Jesus. Disclaimer: What follows is deeply offensive on multiple levels. This quote is taken directly from their website, godhatesfags.com:

> WBC engages in daily peaceful sidewalk demonstrations opposing the homosexual lifestyle of soul-damning, nation-destroying filth. We display large, colorful signs containing Bible words and sentiments, including: GOD HATES FAGS, FAGS HATE GOD, AIDS CURES FAGS, THANK GOD FOR AIDS, FAGS BURN IN HELL, GOD IS NOT MOCKED, FAGS ARE NATURE FREAKS, GOD GAVE FAGS UP, NO SPECIAL LAWS FOR FAGS, FAGS DOOM NATIONS, THANK GOD FOR DEAD SOLDIERS, FAG TROOPS, GOD BLEW UP THE TROOPS, GOD HATES AMERICA, AMERICA IS DOOMED, THE WORLD IS DOOMED, etc.[3]

Make sure to invite them to your next gathering, whether picnic, barbecue, or birthday party—they are loads of fun! This may seem unbelievable, but these people really exist, and there are more like them out there. The picture they paint of Jesus is one of hatred and judgment. It implies a very particular reading of the Scriptures with a particular understanding of Jesus and His mission.

Countless souls have been wounded by this depiction. And these people don't care because their version of Jesus is right. There is a ticker on their website that reads "nanoseconds of sleep that WBC members lose over your opinions and feeeeelllllliiiiiings. – 0." Just in case you thought they might care.

In an effort not to comment much on each version of Jesus beyond describing them and possible outcomes, I will simply say that, of all the versions, this one might grieve me the most.

We frequently see Jesus as if looking through a keyhole, unable or unwilling to see a bigger picture. In fact, the sad truth is we make Him out to be what we want. In short, He looks like us. He carries our wants, wishes, ideas, and leanings with a spiritual spin. This gives us the divine right to feel, act, or think the way we do because Jesus did it that way. He is used to justify our biases and, in turn, becomes nothing more than a caricature of the flavor of the day—our preferred flavor.

The Jesus revealed in the Gospels fits into some of the previously mentioned categories, but there is so much more to Him. Generally, we leave out key details about Jesus from our own version of who He is and was. For instance, nobody seems to like the "I came to bring division" Jesus. I have not seen that on a card at

Christmastime. Or how about the Jesus who said, in the same passage, "I came to bring a sword"? Maybe Walker's idea of Jesus as a ninja fighting off samurai isn't that farfetched, after all!

It's time to broaden our view of Jesus, to expand outward from some of our narrow perceptions. Let's take the blinders off. Let's look beyond what we want to see. For most of us, this will mean looking at some difficult aspects of Jesus that we may tend to avoid. But, if He is speaking to us today, shouldn't we listen to *all* He has to say?

The things Jesus said were directly related to His vocation, and because we already know so much about the beautiful things He said, I would like to focus next on some of the not-so-nice things Jesus said. Once we have those things in mind, we will have a much clearer picture of how we are to live with one another, not just as Christians, but as human beings.

CHAPTER 2
JESUS TWEETS

280 Characters of Savageness and Beatdowns

A narrow perspective on who Christ is could lead us to the idea that Jesus would never say anything mean or make anyone feel bad. It could also make others claim He is a jerk or an alien, as we saw in Chapter 1. People have perpetuated these ideas by the way they talk about Jesus over coffee or through social media. Jesus is "memed" a thousand times supporting Republicans or Democrats, gays or straights, blacks, whites, browns, etc. Each group of people wants to show that Jesus is on their side by using something He said to prove whatever point they want to make. Jesus is also used by those who wish to mock His followers.

All of this grievously misunderstands what God was doing in Christ. To use Jesus to make your point about whatever sociopolitical debate is going on right now is to claim you know Him in an exclusive way. But Jesus isn't there for us to win arguments. He isn't at our disposal for the mic-drop moment. In fact, He refuses to be placed in any category we have for Him.

Jesus showed this every time His disciples or others tried to pigeonhole Him.

"Are you going to be a king?"

"Can we sit at your side?"

We miss out when we do this type of narrow classification. We miss who He truly is, what that means, and how that impacts the way we live. If you believe Jesus is like Santa, you will live a certain way. If you believe in the Westboro Baptist Jesus, you will live a certain way. And the world will look at Him in that certain way *because of you.*

We don't talk about one aspect of Jesus much, and if we do, it is only in specific instances or closed circles. But I believe we need to talk about it openly and freely. *The reality is that Jesus was judgmental.* Jesus was critical of people.

> **The reality is that Jesus was judgmental. Jesus was critical of people. Jesus said things that made people hurt and angry.**

Jesus said things that made people hurt and angry. Are you sure you want this guy on your side in whatever "war" you are waging on the internet? He would likely condemn you just as quickly as He would condemn anyone else! If you remember, He wasn't overly fond of hypocrites.

Social media and the internet didn't exist in the first century, I know. But if they did, it would be interesting to see what Jesus would post, like, follow, share, or write about. Lord knows, Twitter accounts have the opportunity to inflame the world! If Jesus took to Twitter to make a case for some of the things that were important to Him, it would be fascinating. His feed would run wild with followers, retweets, and Twitter wars! People are so brave on social media. Imagine the things they would say!

To paint a complete picture of Jesus, I have taken the liberty of giving Him a Twitter account. Is it a stretch? Maybe. But I want the force of what Jesus said to have an impact on ears inclined to media that didn't exist two thousand years ago. So, what would He tweet? I decided that, since we have these other versions of who Jesus was and is, I would bring to bear a very different Jesus.

It is selective on purpose, and (be sure to note) my commentary is filled with sarcasm. The tweets have been taken from the Gospel of Matthew. Here, Jesus is found laying waste to people with His tongue and pointing out their character defects. Matthew records Jesus calling people names and pronouncing judgment on others on a consistent basis. This is not the Jesus most people want to be with or the Jesus who is fondly remembered. Maybe it's good He didn't have a Twitter account. He was savage. #JudgmentalJesus

Get ready for a healthy dose of sarcasm.

Tweet #1:

If you aren't super-righteous, you won't go to heaven. #GetYourActTogetherPeople

> For I tell you that unless your righteousness surpasses that of the Pharisees and the teachers of the law, you will certainly not enter the kingdom of heaven.
>
> —Matthew 5:20

That's not nice, Jesus. The Pharisees were the "super-righteous." If they can't get into heaven, who can? Anyway, I thought everyone got into heaven, and became angels, and watched over their loved ones with swords and stuff! Especially dogs. (We know where cats wind up.) The idea that one could be more righteous than the Pharisees was a set-up for failure. How could we be expected to do that? Let's look at this together.

The Pharisees were Law keepers. When I say Law, I mean Law with a capital L. This is the Old Testament Law. And the Pharisees not only kept those rules, but they also added over 600 of their own! The Law governed every aspect of a Pharisee's life. It dictated how they ate, slept, did business, and had sex. It wasn't that other groups of Jews weren't concerned with keeping the Law. They were, but it was commonly known that the Pharisees were the enforcers, making sure everyone followed the Law.

Following the Law was presumed to be the path to righteousness. Righteousness was brought about by doing the right thing according to the Law. So when Jesus tells the average Joe that his righteousness needs to exceed that of the Pharisees, you can imagine the collective gasp He must have heard. The Pharisees were more righteous than the typical person, so Jesus is setting everyone up for disaster and hopelessness. Twitter would be ablaze. Media outlets would roll out this story with the talking head, ticker tape, and interviews with "safe space" seekers and experts who say He has it all wrong. This just can't be right.

Tweet #2:

If you call people bad names, you are going to hell. #YouAreATotalMoron

You have heard that it was said to the people long ago, "You shall not murder, and anyone who murders will be subject to judgment." But I tell you that anyone who is angry with a brother or sister will be subject to judgment. Again, anyone who says to a brother or sister, "Raca," is answerable to the court. And anyone who says, "You fool!" will be in danger of the fire of hell.

—Matthew 5:21–22

Clearly, Jesus didn't know people. I mean real people. If He did, He would have never said that if you call people fools, you are in danger of the fire of hell. Doesn't He know that people are idiots and there is no such place as hell? What's with this crazy talk?

I know what it is—He didn't have a Facebook account during the recent presidential election. If He had, Jesus would know there are fools. Loads of them.

And they are not afraid to go online with what they think.

I don't get it, Jesus. What's the big deal with telling the truth, anyway? Some people need to hear they are fools, don't they? What is going on here? And doesn't Jesus know hell is only a metaphor? If hell doesn't exist, there can't be any danger, and if there is no danger, then we can say whatever we want, and Jesus was wrong. Jesus, you're being foolish.

Tweet #3:

If you lust, you are an adulterer. #KeepYourEyesOnYourOwnPaper

> You have heard that it was said, "You shall not commit adultery." But I tell you that anyone who looks at a woman lustfully has already committed adultery with her in his heart.
>
> —Matthew 5:27–28

Jesus called people adulterers for lusting. I guess that means all of us. Yes, even you. In our hyper-sexualized Western world, how are we supposed to keep this from happening? Sex is used to sell *everything*! You can't see a commercial for a burger joint without facing half-naked women enjoying lunch.

Besides, lust isn't bad, right? There's nothing wrong with looking if you don't touch. God wouldn't have made people beautiful if He didn't want us to notice them. And people want to be leered at. No, really, they do, or they wouldn't put themselves out there like that!

Lust doesn't affect anyone but me. How can that be a bad thing?

Tweet #4:

You are all a bunch of hypocrites. #WhyIDontGoToChurch

You hypocrite, first take the plank out of your own eye, and then you will see clearly to remove the speck from your brother's eye.

—Matthew 7:5

One of Jesus' favorite names for people was *hypocrite*. A brief etymology of the word reveals something interesting. It comes from the Greek and is a combination of two words. Spelled phonetically, they are *hupa* and *kreetase*. Hupa means under, and kreetase comes from the word for judgment. Jesus tells people they are under judgment—specifically, their own judgment. *Hypocrite* also referred to actors: those who pretend to be someone they are not. They wear masks. Jesus doesn't like that.

Jesus uses this term to describe people more than once in Matthew (see 6:2, 16; 7:5). Doesn't He know people don't like being called hypocrites? It stings and drives people away. It is offensive! Everyone is a hypocrite in some way. We certainly don't need Him pointing it out. Besides, He's a hypocrite for calling people names when He says we shouldn't do it. So there, Jesus.

Tweet #5:

I hate farm animals. #DogsAndPigsAreStill BetterThanCats

> Do not give dogs what is sacred; do not throw your pearls to pigs. If you do, they may trample them under their feet, and turn and tear you to pieces.
>
> —Matthew 7:6

Speaking of offensive, it isn't exactly PC for Jesus to call someone a dog or a pig, but He does it. He tells His followers not to give sacred or valuable things to farm animals. Nowadays, of course, we find these critters in purses or murses (a man's handbag, in case you didn't know!), hanging over the shoulders of important people in Beverly Hills. Their little heads and snouts poke proudly out of the latest Burberry purse. I don't see those puppies and piglets trampling anyone's valuables, so maybe they aren't all that bad.

Also, this comment from Jesus comes right after He tells people not to judge, so how does He get off doing what He tells us not to do? Isn't that hypocritical?

Tweet #6:

You people suck at praying. #YouAreDoingItAllWrong

> And when you pray, do not be like the hypocrites, for they love to pray standing in the synagogues and on the street corners to be seen by others. ... And when you pray, do not keep on babbling like pagans, for

they think they will be heard because of their many words. Do not be like them.

—Matthew 6:5–8

Jesus mocks the way the "pagans" "babble" when they pray and links them with the heinous hypocrites. Substance over volume, people. God doesn't need all the words; He just wants it done the right way. The sun, tree, sky, plant, and ant worshippers apparently made a lot of noise and said a lot of stuff when they prayed. Maybe they weren't being heard. Stop praying the way everyone else does. Jesus is basically saying, "Start praying with the right heart and with the right motivation. God knows what you are going to say anyway, so don't jam up the heavens with a bunch of words. And, if you get this praying thing wrong, you won't be forgiven." That's really nice, Jesus.

Tweet #7:
People suck. #PeopleSuck

But go and learn what this means: "I desire mercy, not sacrifice." For I have not come to call the righteous, but sinners.

—Matthew 9:13

Jesus calls people evil and sinners in Matthew 7:10 and 9:13. Of course, Jesus is following the strategy found in Chapter 5 of *How to Make Friends and Influence People*. Calling people evil and sinners is a great way to cause people to flock to you. They can't get enough of this stuff. Everyone loves being reminded of how they fall short of perfection, right? Before long, He will have more followers than He knows what to do with. Bring on the guilt and shame!

Doesn't He know that people are basically good? Doesn't He know they are trying? Calling people evil and sinful hurts their feelings. It is really discouraging. If this guy were invited to speak on a college campus, riots and protests would break out! What gives Him the right to say that? No one is perfect. He isn't perfect either! Or, wait—is He?

Tweet #8:

If you don't listen, you're screwed. #CantYouFollowDirections

> But everyone who hears these words of mine and does not put them into practice is like a foolish man who built his house on sand.
>
> —Matthew 7:26

Isn't it convenient? Jesus says you're a fool if you don't listen to Him. Basically, He is the dispenser of all that is good in the world. His way or the highway. But this backs people into a corner. What if you don't like what He says? What if you don't agree?

It really isn't fair for Him to do this. Besides, this is a slippery slope. If you don't follow what I say, you are foolish. Doesn't that make you a fool? But then you are calling people fools. Wait. Aren't you in danger of hell for calling people fools? I guess Jesus is putting

Himself in danger. Maybe Jesus wants to go to hell for another reason.

Tweet #9:

Burial rights are overrated. #YourDeadGrandmaDoesntMatter

> But Jesus told him, "Follow me, and let the dead bury their own dead."
>
> —Matthew 8:22

Jesus says that following Him is a more significant priority than burial rites. How uncaring can you be? This poor guy just wanted to bury his father, but Jesus says no, He is more important. That's crazy talk. I lived with my dad my whole life. He taught me all I know. I just met you. You aren't more important. If my dad died, I would want to bury him and honor him. Isn't that a commandment? Honor your father and your mother? I'm sure of it. How is it honoring to "let the dead bury their dead?" What is with this guy?

Tweet #10:

Jesus really hates farm animals. #NoBaconNoSausage #PorkIsNotTheOtherWhiteMeat

> He said to [the demons], "Go!" So they came out and went into the pigs, and the whole herd rushed down the steep bank into the lake and died in the water.
>
> —Matthew 8:32

He is really all over the place. In this story, Jesus costs a man an entire herd of pigs. I know pigs were unclean animals to the Jews, but really? The pig farmer wasn't Jewish. He didn't have legal restrictions on animals and cleanliness. He was just trying to make a living, raising pigs near a demon-possessed guy. And you think your job is tough!

The farmer probably avoided him at all costs. It would be weird to know there was a possessed guy near where you were hanging out with your animals. How brutal is it that the demons he was trying to avoid cost him the means to make ends meet? Why punish him for some demon-possessed guy? This is taking the pig-hating to a whole new level.

Tweet #11:

Either they deserve it, or they don't. #FireandBrimstoneAreComing #IShakeMyDustyFeetInYourGeneralDirection

> If anyone will not welcome you or listen to your words, leave that home or town and shake the dust off your feet.
>
> —Matthew 10:14

In Matthew 10:5–15, the disciples of Jesus are told not to go to Gentiles or Samaritans. Don't share my good news with those people. I know everyone is supposed to benefit from my message, but it isn't for them. Instead, go to the lost sheep of Israel. When you do, judge whether the home is deserving or undeserving. Offer the undeserving no peace and shake the dust off your feet if you are not welcomed.

The shaking of dust was a sign that doesn't really hold the same weight today. If someone is shaking their foot, it's usually because their foot is asleep or they stepped in something nasty. I guess it's kind of like that last one, actually—shaking the dust off the foot is like saying "You and your land are gross, and I'm not happy I stepped in you."

Jesus goes on to say that, because they didn't receive the disciples well, it will be worse for them than Sodom and Gomorrah. I guess that means fire and brimstone, which is basically like burning sulfur from the sky. So it will be worse than smelly flaming rocks falling upon you. This is the message He wants His disciples to spread.

As if it weren't bad enough, Jesus is telling His followers it's okay in this situation to be judgmental, but not generally speaking. This guy is so confusing!

Tweet #12:

Don't make me the poster child for your peace project. #ImSplittingFamilies

Brother will betray brother to death, and a father his child; children will rebel against their parents and have them put to death. You will be hated by everyone because of me, but the one who stands firm to the end will be saved.

—Matthew 10:21–22

This sounds like the guy you want to have over for dinner, right? Let's make Him the poster child for all the family-first agendas and talk about how He will bring peace to the family and the rest of the world. Nope.

He's drawing a sword (v. 34), which isn't an instrument of peace like a flute or harp. If you decide to follow this guy, you'd better be ready to have your loved ones turn on you. (v. 34–35) "Hurray! Jesus is coming to dinner! This will be a ton of fun! I can't wait to see how our family implodes from His message!"—said no one, ever.

Tweet #13:

If you turn your back on me, I will turn my back on you. #YouCantHaveItBothWays

Whoever acknowledges me before others, I will also acknowledge before my Father in heaven. But whoever disowns me before others, I will disown before my Father in heaven.

—Matthew 10:32–33

This isn't 4th grade. You don't get to talk smack about people and get away with it! If you deny Jesus, He will deny you. Plain and simple. But some people really don't like you, Jesus. What would they think if they knew we were friends?

By the way, have You seen Your people? Not exactly the crowd I want to be lumped in with. Doesn't Peter deny Jesus in Chapter 26 of Matthew? Maybe it's because Peter was really sorry afterward, so everything was okay. What's the deal?

Tweet #14:
Miracles should make a difference. #TurnOrBurn

Then Jesus began to denounce the towns in which most of his miracles had been performed because they did not repent. "Woe to you, Chorazin! Woe to you, Bethsaida! And you, Capernaum, will you be lifted to the heavens? No, you will go down to Hades."

—Matthew 11:20–21

Jesus is willing to denounce entire communities for their lack of repentance. This sounds a bit harsh, don't you think? I mean, come on! That's a lot of people! And there are people in those towns who like You, Jesus. I guess He figured that causing the lame to walk, making the blind see, and freeing demon-possessed people should do the trick. But these folks didn't get it. And not getting it means you go to hell.

That's really uncool. Isn't there some way You can compromise? What if some people didn't see You do the miracles? What if they didn't know anyone who was healed? Jesus says the day of judgment will be more comfortable for the pagan cities than for them. The pagans worship the earth, but we worship Yahweh. It can't be that bad, can it?

Tweet #15:

You can't sit on the fence. #PickASidePeople

> Whoever is not with me is against me, and whoever does not gather with me scatters.
>
> —Matthew 12:30

Really, though? I mean, isn't it possible to do both? Somedays I sow, some days I scatter? We aren't perfect. Jesus needs to relax. Just because I am not actively working with You doesn't mean I'm working against You. Does it? I really hate these false binaries. It isn't black or white. It isn't this or that. It isn't for or against. That just isn't the way people work. Jesus, you really don't understand people at all!

Tweet #16:

Jesus doesn't like poisonous reptiles. #KeepYourForkedTongueInYourHead

> Make a tree good, and its fruit will be good, or make a tree bad and its fruit will be bad, for a tree is recognized by its fruit. You brood of vipers, how can you who are evil say anything good?
>
> —Matthew 12:33–34

A brood of vipers is a family of poisonous snakes ... yikes. Nobody wants to be around poisonous snakes. They are scary. I don't care what Steve Irwin said. They can kill you, and you don't know when they may strike. They don't make good pets. Jesus is right to hate them.

However, calling people a brood of vipers is kinda mean. He condemns the Pharisees because they are evil and can't produce anything good. Like snakes. Seriously, though, snakes are bad. But was every Pharisee bad?

Tweet #17:

Your entire generation is wicked. #NotBostonWicked

Then some of the Pharisees and teachers of the law said to him, "Teacher, we want to see a sign from you." He answered, "A wicked and adulterous generation asks for a sign! But none will be given it except the sign of the prophet Jonah. ... And the final condition of that person is worse than the first. That is how it will be with this wicked generation."

—Matthew 12:38–39, 45

You are wicked. The entire generation is wicked. Not *cool* wicked but *evil* wicked. And adulterous. Basically, the only hope for these folks is to repent in a significant way. The only sign they will get is from Jonah. You can run, but you can't hide. A massive storm is coming. A giant fish (it wasn't a whale, people!) is coming to swallow you. And, like getting sent to your room, you will have three days to think about what you did. You will get puked out, which is really gross. I can't even imagine fish barf. Then you will pout about people responding to the warning they receive, like Jonah did.

Is that what Jesus means? That's a lot to take. Maybe He just means repent. Jesus says this because of their actions and because they wanted to see a sign. (As if He needs to show them more!) Didn't Thomas want to see as well? Jesus makes no bones about it, though. Just as today's older generations condemn millennials, Jesus is happy to cast everyone in the same light. It's pretty negative.

Tweet #18:
I don't like weeds. #NotThatKindOfWeed

The field is the world, and the good seed stands for the people of the kingdom. The weeds are the people of the evil one.

—Matthew 13:38

I know people in Colorado and other places really like weed, but that isn't what we are talking about here. Jesus is calling people weeds that choke stuff out. They grow in the wrong place. People who are in the wrong place are a huge problem; they need to know where they belong. They cause problems and clog up the works. They are more like objects than anything. People like this take away from what is fruitful so that the good fruit can't be grown or appreciated.

When they're discovered, these weed people are uprooted and burned. I guess this is who they are—worthy of being tossed out. This is how Jesus feels about some people. Nice.

Tweet #19:
I only like the good kind. #SomeFishStink

> Once again, the kingdom of heaven is like a net that was let down into the lake and caught all types of fish. When it was full, the fishermen pulled it up on the shore. Then they sat down and collected the good fish in baskets, but threw the bad away. This is how it will be at the end of the age. The angels will come and separate the wicked from the righteous and throw them into the blazing furnace, where there will be weeping and gnashing of teeth.
>
> —Matthew 13:47–50

The end of the age is going to go really poorly for some fish. This isn't a family barbecue Jesus describes here. It sounds like a lot of suffering. Despite the fact that many fish were caught in the same net, the fishermen (who made *them* God, anyway?) are the ones who decide which are good and bad. Hope they like groupers.

Jesus is obviously referring to people here, not fish. Maybe He doesn't like groupers. In any event, bad fish and bad people get the big torch. Angels will be the ones to sort things out. I'm not sure I would want to argue with one of them about my merits.

Tweet #20:

You are going the wrong way! #DontDriveWithThatGuy

> He replied, "Every plant that my heavenly Father has not planted will be pulled up by the roots. Leave them; they are blind guides. If the blind lead the blind, both will fall into a pit."
>
> —Matthew 15:13–14

It's generally accepted that having a guide who has been where you are going is a good plan, especially if the road ahead is steep and unknown. However, if the guide is blind and you are blind too, it may not be a good thing. Jesus doesn't like the Pharisees as guides and doesn't seem to care for those who follow them either.

It's like watching a YouTube video when you know what is going to happen. They are going to fall into a pit … keep watching … it's hilarious! Oh man, I love that video!

Tweet #21:

Peter, you are dumb. #DumbAsARock

> Peter said, "Explain the parable to us." "Are you still so dull?" Jesus asked them. "Don't you see that whatever enters the mouth goes into the stomach and then out of the body?"
>
> —Matthew 15:15–16

It would be tough being Jesus' friend. He leveled criticism at everyone, even His buddies. Poor Peter is just trying to figure out what's going on, and Jesus creams him. Can you hear the sarcasm in His voice? "Are you still so dull?" He could have said "stupid." It has the same effect.

Imagine the scene: Jesus is at a party (He went to them often), and He is introducing His disciples. "And here's Matthew; he was a tax collector, good with money, sharp guy. And this is Peter. He is duller than a rock. Hey, wait. Rock. That has a nice ring to it!"

Tweet #21:

You are a dog, and you know it! #DogsEatGrossStuff #NotPC

A Canaanite woman from that vicinity came to him, crying out, "Lord, Son of David, have mercy on me! My daughter is demon-possessed and suffering terribly." Jesus did not answer a word. So, his disciples came to him and urged him, "Send her away, for she keeps crying out after us." He answered, "I was sent only to the lost sheep of Israel." The woman came and knelt before him. "Lord, help me!" she said. He replied, "It is not right to take the children's bread and toss it to the dogs." "Yes, it is, Lord," she said. "Even the dogs eat the crumbs that fall from their master's table."

—Matthew 15:22–27

Of all the names Jesus calls people, *dog* has to be one of the worst. I used to think being a dog would be cool because you could do whatever you wanted. You could eat when you wanted, you could sleep wherever, and you wouldn't have to worry about those pesky bathrooms. Then I saw a dog on my wife's family ranch. It changed my mind. It ate some seriously gross things. I won't go into what I saw, but let's just say it wasn't table scraps (insert shudder here). Upon closer inspection, the dog wasn't really clean either. It had burs in its hair, it was covered with a thin layer of dust, and it carried an off-putting aroma.

Jesus calls the woman a dog. I don't know if He meant a ranch dog, but I think the images it brings up are close enough. If that happened today, He would lose all His sponsors. CEOs would put out statements about how He doesn't reflect the values of their companies. He would be uninvited to speaking engagements as organizations scrambled to put distance between them and Him. Cancellations for parties and TV appearances would pile up. His Twitter feed would get loaded with negative responses, and His followers would drop by the thousands. It's not nice to call people four-legged critters. Especially poor ladies in need.

Postscript:

The good thing is, all of this would be captured on video. The lady would receive hundreds of sympathy comments, a GoFundMe site would be set up, and people would give thousands to try to undo the pain Jesus caused. Until, of course, He does it to the next person.

Tweet #22:

You are the worst! #TheAccuser #PeterTheAccuser

> From that time on Jesus began to explain to his disciples that he must go to Jerusalem and suffer many things at the hands of the elders, the chief priests and the teachers of the law and that he must be killed and on the third day be raised to life. Peter took him aside and began to rebuke him. "Never, Lord!" he said. "This shall never happen to you!" Jesus turned and said to Peter, "Get behind me, Satan! You are a stumbling block to me; you do not have in mind the concerns of God, but merely human concerns."
>
> —Matthew 16:21–23

Jesus saved the best for last. Calling Peter "Satan" sets the standard for name-calling. It doesn't get any lower, or better, depending on how you look at it. "You are the deceiver. You are the one who sows discord. You are the one who plots against the good. You are the one who stands against all that Jesus is doing. You're like the one who deceived Adam and Eve and started this whole mess." All this because he didn't want Jesus to get killed. That is a terrible name to call someone for trying to care for you. He was only trying to help. Gosh.

So, what are we to get from all of this name-calling and sarcasm?

#JudgmentalJesus was harsh! He said mean things and called people names! His Twitter account would be on fire! Can you imagine the wars He would have ignited? This Twitter-loving Jesus wouldn't care about people's feelings. He provided no safe spaces and no participation trophies. He laid people to waste!

While these tweets are fictitious (and hopefully a bit funny), they make a point. Jesus was judgmental. Everyone was in His crosshairs. He held nothing back when it came to telling it like it is.

Think about the ground He covered. As far as the religious leaders went, He called them blind guides, hypocrites, a brood of vipers, and so on. He was unhappy with these guys. For the traditionalists, He called into question deeply held customs like burial and roles within the family. Those who would like to have their cake and eat it too—He told them to pick a side. Not one group was outside the scope of Jesus' scornful glance.

This isn't your grandma's Jesus! #NotMyJesus

Why is He like this? What is He hoping to accomplish? And if He was so mean and judgmental, why are we still following Him two thousand years later? Most of us understand there was more to Jesus than these tweets. But we do tend to mainly focus on our favorite version without much reference to this judgmental side of Him.

People who speak this kind of truth have a way of exposing things in us we don't like to show. It wasn't as though the disciples were outside His venomous range. Peter gets called Satan, for Pete's sake. (See what I did there?) If those closest to Him were not exempt, no one was.

While this makes for great copy, it cost Jesus dearly. Those in power didn't take kindly to being called on the carpet like that. So what did they do? The Pharisees, Sadducees, and temple leaders made a point of trying to kill Jesus.

Then the leading priests and the older Jewish leaders had a meeting at the palace where the high priest lived. The high priest's name was Caiaphas. In the meeting they tried to find a way to arrest and kill Jesus without anyone knowing what they were doing. They planned to arrest Jesus and kill him. They said, "We cannot arrest Jesus during Passover. We don't want the people to become angry and cause a riot."

—Matthew 26:3–5

We know how that ended. They succeeded. But not without help. It wasn't legal for the Jews to kill Jesus for the charges they made against Him, and they had thorny sociopolitical issues they had to dance around. So they came to Pilate.

Pilate had a delicate balance to maintain as well. He had to please Rome and Caesar, satisfy those he governed (they weren't too happy about him already), and figure out a way to keep a riot and rebellion from erupting. All this at the most pivotal time of the Jewish year: Passover.

Passover is the time when Jews commemorate their plunder of and flight from the Egyptians. It's a time Jews look back upon with fondness—despite the bitter herbs eaten at the meal—because of how God acted on their behalf. Israel was delivered (and born, in many respects) at the Passover. God pronounced judgment on Israel's enemies at the Passover. All those flies, frogs, blood, and death were brought down upon their oppressors.

To say Passover was a nationalistic holiday would be putting it mildly, and Pilate knew it. He was genuinely caught between a rock and a hard place. To not appease the Jewish leaders would mean rebellion and bloodshed.

It would also bring the stare of the emperor down upon him. To appease the people involved the death of a man he found undeserving of such a punishment.

However, Jesus was a problem for Rome. He didn't deny certain titles others gave Him, and He placed some upon Himself by His actions and teaching. He didn't deny being the Messiah, and He didn't deny being the King of the Jews. Rome wouldn't accept a messiah for the Jews. There would be no deliverance, no pillar of fire, no cloud protecting and leading them. It wouldn't tolerate a king either. There was only one lord, and it wasn't Jesus. Kings were appointed by Rome as a way to ensure the peace, keep order, and prevent rebellion. The Herodians were the kings. Each had a cool name: Herod the Great, Herod Archelaus, and Herod Antipas. Jesus wasn't a Herod. Any claim to kingship confronted Rome in both regards.

So Pilate did what he had to do.

While Jesus didn't tweet, He did push buttons. And the buttons pushed back, leading to His crucifixion. What they didn't know and couldn't understand was that Jesus was more than a great teacher. He was more than a would-be Messiah. The following week would provide more than enough evidence for that.

CHAPTER 3
THE JUDGMENTAL JESUS #NOTMYJESUS

Who does this guy think He is?

Jesus would have been pretty scary to be around. He called it like He saw it, and He didn't pull any punches. It was clear He had no problem pointing out the flaws in people. In general, when people act like that, they are trying to cover up their insecurities—if others feel small or unwanted, they may feel better about themselves. Is that what Jesus is doing here? If it is, we have a big problem. God in the flesh is a neurotic, insecure juvenile? I'm glad that isn't the case.

Jesus was a friend of tax collectors and sinners. Matthew 9 shows Him eating with them. Even the Gospel of Matthew was written by a tax collector. Why would these people want to hang out with such a judgmental guy? One of the arguments I have heard is that Jesus was judging the elite, the rulers and church leaders, not the ordinary people. If that is true, then only the leaders were hypocrites and adulterers? I don't think so.

Jesus held His judgments from no one. Maybe it is because the sinners just loved it when Jesus "stuck it" to the Pharisees and other religious leaders. Sure, this would have been amusing on some level, but something far more serious was happening here. His eye was on them as well. Again, in Matthew 9, Jesus says it is the "sick," referring to those He was hanging out with, who need a doctor. These simple ideas, however, don't quite paint the full picture.

To help get a better view, let us now turn our attention to what we have traditionally heard or known about Jesus. Not just the 8-pound, 6-ounce infant Jesus of Christmas, but the bearded—not to mention, loving, compassionate, and forgiving—Jesus.

Jesus—Messiah

Jesus, in Matthew's Gospel, comes to us by way of genealogy. Matthew is keen on making sure his readers know the Jewish roots of the Christ child. He is placed in line with the "greats" of the Jewish faith: Abraham and David. From the beginning of the story, we are to see Jesus playing a pivotal role in what God has done with the Jewish people.

This lineage is then linked to prophecy about the Messiah. Messiah is one of the titles Jesus carried. In human terms, He would have been "Jesus bar Joseph" (son of Joseph). His last name wasn't Christ. Christ comes from *Xristos*, Greek for Anointed One. Both Greek speakers and Hebrew speakers described Jesus this way. In Hebrew, the title was *Mashiyach*. This is where the word Messiah comes from. It was a loaded term. Many have claimed it, but only One has fulfilled it.

Much has been written about first-century Jewish Messianic expectation that will not be repeated here. Read *New Testament People of God* by NT Wright for an excellent description.[4] A basic summary is that the Messiah will

- Overthrow Israel's enemies
- Restore Israel to be a great nation
- Be a great leader/king like David
- Restore the temple

Jesus fulfilled these expectations in ways that were unexpected and far more thorough than any could have imagined. While He looked nothing like David, His function as Messiah was undeniable, and those who followed Him (even those who hated Him) knew it.

Rome

Israel had more than one enemy during the first century, but her greatest enemy was Rome. These outsiders conquered the area roughly seventy years before Jesus came on the scene. This was a problem for many reasons. So much of Jewish identity had to do with the land of Israel. The land has always been a central theme for the people of God. Think about the garden of Eden. Think about the curse on the land and having to toil and deal with thorns. Think about the flood cleansing the land. Think about the promises of God about land and fruitfulness. God promised a land flowing with milk and honey. God promised His people abundance.

The Babylonian exile was one of the lowest—maybe *the* lowest—time in Jewish history. They were separated from their land. They were separated from the promises of God, and their identity as God's people took a significant blow. Rome invading the land had a similar impact. It would have been a close second to exile. The Roman presence would have been a constant reminder of the Jews' status as a defeated people. With every tax payment they made, every soldier they walked past, every symbol of Caesar they saw, their hatred would have grown.

There was no way a military revolt would overthrow Rome. The Jews tried, shortly after Jesus' resurrection, but it didn't go well. How, then, would the Messiah conquer Rome? When considering what the anticipated leader would be like, the Jews believed the military-king-like Messiah would somehow invoke God's presence, perhaps in miraculous ways, and God would reveal Himself. Maybe it would be through walls falling, angels descending, pillars of fire, or the enemy suddenly becoming blind. Somehow, some way, Rome would get what was coming to it.

The power of Rome lay in its army, culture, religion, structure, and government. How could you overcome that? The only way, it turns out, was through the defeat of death, sin, and hell itself.

Jesus spoke and taught about another Kingdom. It wasn't of this earth, but it was in the hearts and minds of humankind. This Kingdom could pay taxes to Caesar, follow Rome's laws, willingly submit to injustice, have her subjects tortured and killed, but not be defeated. This was a different kind of Messiah King, and it was a different kind of Kingdom—one that would far outstrip Rome in years and adherents.

A Great Nation

In the annals of Jewish memory, there was a time when Israel was a great and powerful nation. There were two kingdoms: the northern kingdom, Israel, and the southern kingdom, Judah. Israel was the more significant, but when with the two kingdoms combined, a broad swath of the Eastern Mediterranean was ruled by the Jews. The kingdoms of the Philistines, Edomites, Moabites, and Ammonites put pressure on her, but although they battled back and forth from roughly 100 BCE, Israel or Judah always had a strong presence in the area. Outside Israel and Judah, there were, of course, much larger and more powerful kingdoms and empires.

The Babylonians and Assyrians, as well as Rome, had their way with the Israelites. So, when we think of a "great and powerful nation," it has to be seen from two perspectives. One is by today's standards. Israel's kingdom, from our modern viewpoint with what we now know of the world, was relatively small and unimportant. Compared to the thousand-year reign of Rome, what is Israel? However, from the second perspective (Israel's own), they were a significant player on the block. Despite the fact that the neighborhood was relatively small, Israel, like a Middle Eastern wolverine, fought these giant empires and local neighbors with ferocity and even some success.

The Messiah was expected to return her to the glory days of importance, influence, and military strength. Did Jesus do these things for Israel? Not exactly.

In Genesis 12, God gives Abram this promise:

> The Lord had said to Abram, "Go from your country, your people and your father's household to the land I will show you.
>
> "I will make you into a great nation, and I will bless you; I will make your name great, and you will be a blessing. I will bless those who bless you, and whoever curses you I will curse, and all peoples on earth will be blessed through you."

The Messiah would help fulfill this promise. But how? This seemed especially difficult in Jesus' day, considering they were an occupied people.

This coveted idea of becoming a great nation—being blessed and a blessing as well as making Abram's name great—came with the understanding of political, cultural, military, and religious influence. It was also tied to the land.

When Jesus talked about God's Kingdom, He spoke of it being present. It was here and now. Jesus was inaugurating the Kingdom and revealing signposts to it as well as showing what it is like. The miracles, teaching, and redemptive work were all part of the Kingdom of God. These things demarcated the people of God as well. It was these people in this Kingdom in whom God was at work.

The promise to Abram was that all peoples on earth would be blessed through him. God never intended His reach to stop at a sociopolitical border. His intent wasn't only for Jews, but also Gentiles (non-Jews). When Jesus redefines God's Kingdom in and through His life, death, and resurrection, the true vision of a great nation comes into focus.

This nation is not political—it's about the hearts and minds of God's people, who will be of many skin tones, lands, languages, and time periods extending from well before Jesus to at least two thousand years after. That is quite the nation! This really does make Abraham's descendants as numerous as the number of the stars. Israel, through the Messiah, has become a great nation again! No geopolitical boundaries can contain her.

A Great Leader Like David

David is unanimously considered the greatest leader in Israel's history. So much about him shouts the story of the nation itself. The smallest, youngest, least likely of all sons becomes the king. Israel plays the underdog role in similar ways. Despite her size and influence, she is chosen by God. When God calls Samuel to anoint a new king, He sends him to the house of Jesse. After viewing all his sons and hearing nothing from the Lord, this happens.

So he asked Jesse, "Are these all the sons you have?"

"There is still the youngest," Jesse answered. "He is tending the sheep."

Samuel said, "Send for him; we will not sit down until he arrives."

So he sent for him and had him brought in. He was glowing with health and had a fine appearance and handsome features.

Then the Lord said, "Rise and anoint him; this is the one."

So Samuel took the horn of oil and anointed him in the presence of his brothers, and from that day on the Spirit of the Lord came powerfully upon David. Samuel then went to Ramah.

—1 Samuel 16:11–13

David was a boy and a shepherd. He becomes an incredible warrior and king. The Messiah would have these dual functions: shepherd and warrior-king. It is the best of both worlds. Someone who can care for others but fight for them as well. Someone who can kill enemies who threaten but also tend to the wounds of the sheep. One eye on the beloved and one eye on the enemy.

This Messiah would help lead Israel back to prominence through His dual functions of shepherd and warrior-king. Tall order? Let's look at how it all played out.

Jesus comes from a small, no-name family and a backwater part of the nation. Nazareth wasn't exactly the epicenter of culture and trade. It is hardly mentioned in the Gospels at all. When it is, it isn't with awe and wonder.

"Nazareth! Can anything good come from there?" Nathanael asked.

"Come and see," said Philip (John 1:46).

His birth is in a manger, on the run from authorities. Unlikely stuff for the Christ. This is what Isaiah prophesied about Him:

For to us, a child is born, to us, a son is given, and the government will be on his shoulders.

And he will be called Wonderful Counselor, Mighty God, Everlasting Father, Prince of Peace. Of the greatness of his government and peace, there will be no end.

He will reign on David's throne and over his kingdom, establishing and upholding it with justice and righteousness from that time on and forever. The zeal of the Lord Almighty will accomplish this.

Jesus' early life is hardly what you would expect from a Messiah. Further in Isaiah, it says,

You who bring good news to Zion, go up on a high mountain. You who bring good news to Jerusalem, lift up your voice with a shout, lift it up, do not be afraid; say to the towns of Judah, "Here is your God!"

See, the Sovereign Lord comes with power, and he rules with a mighty arm.

See, his reward is with him, and his recompense accompanies him.

He tends his flock like a shepherd:

He gathers the lambs in his arms and carries them close to his heart; he gently leads those that have young.

Jesus would do all of this, just not in the way commonly expected.

He Would Restore the Temple

The temple was the center of Jewish life. God's presence resided in the Holy of Holies. Sacrifices were offered there. Economies sprang up around and inside the temple based on those sacrifices. All faithful Jews made the pilgrimage each year to the temple to worship at the Passover. The temple and Jewish identity were inextricably tied.

The first temple was attributed to King Solomon. It was a grand building proclaiming Israel's greatness to anyone who visited. It was destroyed by the Babylonians when Judah was defeated in 587 BCE. The second temple, built on the same spot as the first, functioned similarly. It was the place where heaven touched the earth, God came to humankind, and people could see there was a great God in Israel. But it wasn't functioning that way in the first century.

Sacrifices were offered, prayers were said, sacred texts were read. All of the outward signs were there, but Jesus talked about how the temple and Israel would be judged. In fact, that is part of what got Him killed. Temple leaders heard Jesus predict the temple's destruction (which did occur in 70 CE), and they didn't like it much. He also talked about His temple, and how it would rise up in three days. What do Jesus' body and the temple of Jerusalem have to do with one another, anyway?

Jews expected God's glory to return to the temple. It became a symbol of rebellion, though, instead of peace. It was the center of Jewish identity instead of the headwaters of God's grace and mercy.

When Jesus cleansed the temple, He shut it down. After spending the majority of His life outside Jerusalem,

He entered the city for a final showdown with the religious authorities. Upon arriving at the temple, he found it full of merchants selling items for sacrifice and changing money. Instead of prayer, he found business. So, he did what any sound-minded person would do. He tipped over the tables, scattered the goods, and drove everyone out! He judged it (there He goes again with the judging!) as only God could. The entire system was condemned as corrupt and ineffective.

So how was the temple restored? The Jews focused on the building, but Jesus focused on where God resides. God would now live with His people by His Spirit. The "temple" is now with men in a new way. Restored and liberated, the temple has a new function and a new way of doing business.

Jesus was a Shepherd-Messiah. God's promises were fulfilled in and through Him. This was who He was *and* how He functioned.

There are divine, royal, military, and shepherding components to the Messiah. Jesus fits the bill for each of these, but not in the way it was expected. Mathew's Gospel records Him functioning in each of these capacities, but like the narrow perspectives described in Chapter 1, they are incomplete in and of themselves. Jesus isn't what we make Him out to be. He is more than that. And He was judgmental.

Judge

Because of who He is and how He functions, He has every right to be judgmental.

No one in human history can claim and live out the titles that Jesus can. He is both human and divine, taking a unique seat. He can judge. Why? Because Jesus is *the* Judge. Some worship communities declare each week in the Creed that He will come again "to judge the living and the dead." Jesus is comfortable judging people because He has every right to do so. His title, function, and very nature make this clear. This is why Matthew records Jesus judging so much. It is part of His role and who He is. We shouldn't expect anything less from Him.

Because Jesus is the Judge, all the pictures we looked at—such as Nice Guy Jesus and Santa Jesus—at the beginning of our text were incomplete. They are made in our image, a reflection of what we want God to do or who we want Him to be, usually because we have left out the judgmental side. I am grateful Jesus refuses to be put into those boxes. They are only part of a mosaic that makes up the image of God With Us.

To be fair, the disciples struggled with this as well. It wasn't as if they had a complete picture of Him from the get-go. They knew Him as a man, but slowly, like the dawn breaking, came to an understanding that He was so much more.

When Jesus came to the region of Caesarea Philippi, he asked his disciples, "Who do people say the Son of Man is?" They replied, "Some say John the Baptist; others say Elijah; and still others, Jeremiah or one of the prophets." "But what about you?" he asked. "Who do you say I am?"

Simon Peter answered, "You are the Messiah, the Son of the living God."

Jesus replied, "Blessed are you, Simon son of Jonah, for this was not revealed to you by flesh and blood, but by my Father in heaven. And I tell you that you are Peter, and on this rock, I will build my church, and the gates of Hades will not overcome it. I will give you the keys of the kingdom of heaven; whatever you bind on earth will be bound in heaven, and whatever you loose on earth will be loosed in heaven." Then he ordered his disciples not to tell anyone that he was the Messiah.

—Matthew 16:13–20

This happens in Chapter 16 of Matthew! A lot happens between Chapters 1 and 15, but this is huge. Peter's confession means the cat is out of the bag. However, the disciples are told not to tell others. To those not in Jesus' inner circle, His identity wasn't self-evident. If those closest to Him had trouble fully understanding, imagine what the crowds thought!

Just because Peter confessed Jesus as the Christ didn't mean Peter had reached a state of perfection. Right after his confession, Jesus calls him Satan, remember? There's a lesson there. Just because you know who He is doesn't mean everything works well. In Matthew's Gospel, demons know who Jesus is. It doesn't go well for them, right?

What about after Jesus' resurrection? There was still confusion. Was He a ghost? A spirit? How do we describe Jesus post-resurrection? There is only one phrase that works: new creation. There are no existing categories to describe someone with a body that eats, talks, and feels, yet travels distances in an instant, appears out of nowhere, and is not bound by walls, time, or space. Crazy, huh? Yet that's what we see in the Scriptures.

Jesus continued to call people to repentance even after His resurrection. For instance, while he was still a fierce Pharisee, Saul traveled on the road to Damascus from Jerusalem to bring more Christians to justice, and this is when Jesus appeared.

> Meanwhile, Saul was still breathing out murderous threats against the Lord's disciples. He went to the high priest and asked him for letters to the synagogues in Damascus, so that if he found any there who belonged to the Way, whether men or women, he might take them as prisoners to Jerusalem. As he neared Damascus on his journey, suddenly a light from heaven flashed around him. He fell to the ground and heard a voice say to him, "Saul, Saul, why do you persecute me?"
>
> "Who are you, Lord?" Saul asked.
>
> "I am Jesus, whom you are persecuting," he replied. "Now get up and go into the city, and you will be told what you must do."
>
> The men traveling with Saul stood there speechless; they heard the sound but did not see anyone. Saul got up from the ground, but when he opened his eyes, he could see nothing. So they led him by the hand into Damascus. For three days he was blind and did not eat or drink anything.
>
> —Acts 9:1–9

Jesus changed Saul's heart, his mind, and his name. He was now called Paul, and he is the author of most of the New Testament. He made some pretty fantastic claims. One of which is that he learned the gospel from Jesus.

> I want you to know, brothers and sisters, that the gospel I preached is not of human origin. I did not receive it from any man, nor was I taught it; rather, I received it by revelation from Jesus Christ. ... But when God, who set me apart from my mother's womb and called me by his grace, was pleased to reveal his Son in me so that I might preach him among the Gentiles, my immediate response was not to consult any human being. I did not go up to Jerusalem to see those who were apostles before I was, but I went into Arabia. Later I returned to Damascus. Then after three years, I went up to Jerusalem to get acquainted with Cephas and stayed with him fifteen days. I saw none of the other apostles—only James, the Lord's brother. I assure you before God that what I am writing you is no lie.
>
> —Galatians 1:11–20

Paul helped both Jews and Gentile have a much better picture of who Jesus was, just as I've done with this book. (I hope you are laughing!) He was from Tarsus (think Turkey), a Roman citizen, a Jew by religion, and he was subsequently sent to the Gentiles (non-Jews). He was the perfect man for the job of carrying the good news of Jesus' Lordship from Jerusalem to the rest of the world. His words about Jesus are some of the most important written. And, notice, when he wrote to encourage believers about who Jesus was, he didn't shy away from Jesus being Judge.

"For we must all appear before the judgment seat of Christ, so that each one may be recompensed for his deeds in the body, according to what he has done, whether good or bad" (2 Corinthians 5:10).

"This will take place on the day when God judges people's secrets through Jesus Christ, as my gospel declares" (Romans 2:16).

These are just snippets, of course. The totality of the New Testament bears a much greater witness than these. But perhaps I digress. Let's let Matthew have a say.

"Jesus said to them, 'Truly I tell you, at the renewal of all things, when the Son of Man sits on his glorious throne, you who have followed me will also sit on twelve thrones, judging the twelve tribes of Israel'" (Matthew 19:28).

Jesus was judgmental because He was, in part, a judge. He was and will be the one to whom all will give an account. Not a Twitter account, but an accounting of where we stand with Him!

Now, nobody likes to be judged. It feels awful when someone tells you that you don't measure up. Whether it is a low test score, a low credit score, or a boss who doesn't promote you for perceived lack of ability or skills, judgment sucks. Feeling like a failure isn't on anyone's top ten list of fun things. No one says, "The most significant moments in my life were when my child was born, when I got married, and when that idiot boss overlooked me." This is how we feel when judged.

It is especially painful when the judgment is justified. We like to live with our delusions about ourselves and our world. They are comfortable and nice. When someone disrupts them with truth—not their version, but what we know is right and have been denying—the pain is excruciating. The loss of illusion can be devastating. Imagine telling your mother-in-law you *don't* like her meatloaf, the one she makes every time you visit because she thinks you love it. (In case you are wondering, my mother-in-law's meatloaf is good.) My point is, feelings of disappointment, betrayal, shame, and stupidity come hard and fast on the heels of judgment.

> My point is, feelings of disappointment, betrayal, shame, and stupidity come hard and fast on the heels of judgment.

When they do, we usually deflect. It is easy to try to find flaws in the person who judges. "Who died and made you God?" Probably not the best question to fire at Jesus. Similar sentiments are found in phrases like, "Well, you aren't perfect either!" or maybe "What gives you the right to judge?" Again, these questions are better left for someone other than Jesus. We can find hypocrisy in those who make judgments because we see them doing the same thing. If we can make it about the person leveling the judgment instead of our own behavior, we can feel the sting a bit less. However, it doesn't change the fact that someone looked into our lives and made a correct judgment about us, our actions, or motives—and it hurts.

King David didn't always model great behavior. Things like rape, murder, and deceit aren't high on the list of moral achievements. But he did showcase some humility in the Psalms when it came to being judged: "Let the righteous strike me; it shall be a kindness. Let him rebuke me; it shall be as excellent oil; let my head not refuse it" (Psalm 141:5).

Being willing to receive a message you don't want to hear can be a game-changer. David describes it as kindness and excellent oil. In other words, these judgments are a blessing. Why? Because they do away with falsehood and pretense. They cut through hypocrisy and the masks we wear. This is a blessing to those interacting with us because they can finally see what is true, not the front we put in place. And it is a blessing to us because we no longer have to hold the mask up, making sure no one sees behind it.

The Proverbs say "faithful are the wounds of a friend" and "he who receives correction is prudent" (also see Proverbs 15:5 and 9:8–9).

These judgments are meant for our good. From them, we can make an entirely new framework for viewing the world. They don't hinder us but unleash us in ways we never knew they could.

This is what Jesus is trying to do with His truth-telling-name-calling-savageness. He is trying to free people from sin, hell, and death, as well as from living a false life. That false life is a sign or marker of everything Jesus is trying to eradicate. Because of His judgment, people can truly understand their position—relationally, spiritually, emotionally, and socially—and from there, make a move. You will never know you are a hypocrite unless you find out, and Jesus is happy to show you. You will never know you have been included, grafted into the outworking of God's purposes in the world, unless you first understand that you are an outsider, like a dog.

This is why Jesus judged. He didn't do it to be a jerk. He didn't do it to make people feel bad. He didn't do it to prove how right He was. He didn't do it to show people how smart He was or that He could win some argument. Jesus judged to free people. He had the title, the vocation, the power, and the willingness to do what it took to release people enslaved to themselves and to hell, sin, and death.

Hopefully, this is all coming into the

Jesus judged to free people.

light for you. Any picture we paint of Jesus, any mosaic we carefully craft of His character and action, that doesn't include how judgmental He was is woefully incomplete. In fact, it misses His Messianic function altogether. The Messiah's chief purpose is for deliverance and saving. That is precisely what Jesus did. How He did it was the most unlikely way possible—but it was undeniably effective.

No one expected the Messiah to live a sinless life. No one expected the Messiah to defy Rome and die, let alone rise again. No one thought that making Israel a great nation would mean salvation for the entire world. But this is what happened: deliverance, and so much more!

Time to take a big breath of fresh air and sigh with me!

In the Scriptures, especially Paul's letters, the key word *therefore* appears often. When studying Paul's work, it is critical to ask this question: "What is the *therefore* there for?" The word generally functions to wrap up an entire section, thought, or argument. Basically, it says, "Based on everything I have said before, look at what I am saying now."

We are now at the *therefore* of this book.

Therefore, because of who Jesus was and is, we can live very different lives. They don't have to be dominated by world events, our emotions, or our past. Jesus transcends those things and redefines them in light of His work. We can live without shame or guilt. We can live with confidence, knowing our Shepherd-King has things under control. Jesus' life, death, and resurrection shape not only the afterlife but also our here and now.

You may be saying to yourself, "Okay, okay, Jesus died for me, I get it." But, hopefully, you are seeing there is so much more going on. Because He is judgmental, He frees us from the need to judge. We are freed to behave in the way He calls us to behave.

We don't have to live or look like the rest of the world because of who He is. The question now is, how do we do it?

CHAPTER 4

HOUSTON, WE HAVE A PROBLEM.

Objectifying People and Fighting Our Culture

Know your role.

Dwayne Johnson made a name for himself, not on the football field as he expected, but in the professional wrestling ring. His name was "The Rock." He brought smack talk to another level. He could insult people in a variety of ways, and his monologues are the stuff of legend. One of his catchphrases was *"Know your role!"* He insisted that those around him were inferior and encouraged them to know their role, which was quite obviously subservient to his.

This happens outside the wrestling ring as well. A quick look at social media gives a glimpse of folks taking sides on all sorts of issues. The keyboard warriors lob shots at those who are different from them as if they are "the anointed." People happily take up a role they weren't asked to assume and aren't always welcomed to take.

In many ways, Christians today could use this message. Sometimes, I think Jesus would tweet "Know your role!" because we get it all wrong. Christians in North America have been busy trying to save our culture or return it to some perceived glory days. Yet the effort to cling to the past or not give up on our "Christian roots" is a mistake.

The Founding Fathers of the United States didn't follow Jesus the way we do today. Looking at them through our modern lenses and assuming they had the same walk, priorities, and desires as people in the 21st century is a great mistake. In general, they were deists: people who believed in God and, maybe, believed in Jesus. However, the 17th- and 18th-century version of that looks very different than today. Specifically, U.S. Founding Fathers had slaves. They likely treated their slaves like any other slave owners. To most 21st-century folks, it's not okay to have slaves. That is just one example of how trying to recapture a glory-filled past just doesn't work. It wasn't all glory.

People will argue that today is terrible because things aren't the way they were when we were kids. Many will opine about being gone all day as youngsters with their parents only having a general idea of where they were— when the street lights came on, it was time to come home. Despite the freedoms I experienced as a child, I have teenagers now, and I would be very uncomfortable with those scenarios playing out with them.

I once asked a man who was lamenting the past when would be a good time to return to? When were the best days of the U.S.? We walked through the century by decade.

1990s – Clinton Scandal, first Gulf War
1980s – AIDS, Iran-Contra
1970s – Vietnam, Watergate
1960s – Vietnam, Segregation
1950s – McCarthyism, Cold War
1940s – World War II, Japanese Internment
1930s – The Great Depression
1920s – Isolationism, Prohibition, Mafia
1910s – World War I
1900s – Advanced Industrialism, Wage Slavery

There wasn't a place where we could land that would make everything okay. Each day and every age have their pros and cons. We mourn loss and hope for something better or we like what we had, but there is no going back and trying to "recover" some sense of our past. This approach is not helping us move forward.

We clearly live in a post-Christian world. Christianity and its morals are not the dominant worldview in the West. Not that there was ever a pristine example of Western Christian faith, but there was at least a religious veneer. People attended church, God was often mentioned, and public prayer wasn't frowned upon but rather expected. These things, however, do not a Christian country make. And that's a good thing. Christianity was never meant to be a dominant socioeconomic force. Since Theodosius made Christianity the official religion of Rome (Constantine gets credit for this, but he only legalized Christianity), we have been dealing with the consequences, both good and bad. But just because the appearance is there doesn't mean it's real.

If our role isn't to "retake" America, then, what is it? What are Christians to do with increasing secularization and infringement upon Christian values and worldviews?

Many people organize in a way similar to the first-century Jews. To deal with the crushing weight of Rome and her rule, the Jews responded by falling into four general categories: the Essenes, the Sadducees, the Pharisees, and the Zealots.

The Essenes decided the best thing to do was withdraw from society. They lived on the fringes of society. They decided the best way to bring about the Kingdom of God was to remove themselves and live according to their own laws and practices.

You might see Christians behaving this way today. It is almost a bunker mentality—they hide in an effort not to be tainted by the world. Maybe it's homeschooling or small group worship, but the plan is to withdraw from the bigger picture.

The problem with this scenario is that it flies in the face of Jesus' teaching. In Matthew 5:13–16, He said this:

> "You are the salt of the earth. But if the salt loses its saltiness, how can it be made salty again? It is no longer good for anything, except to be thrown out and trampled underfoot. You are the light of the world. A town built on a hill cannot be hidden. Neither do people light a lamp and put it under a bowl. Instead, they put it on its stand, and it gives light to everyone in the house. In the same way, let your light shine before others, that they may see your good deeds and glorify your Father in heaven."

Living like an Essene isn't an option for a people whose God loved the world. Our whole purpose is to reveal Jesus to the world. The love He has for the world is the love we are to continue to embody.

The Sadducees were a group of religious and political leaders who differed from the Pharisees in crucial areas. They believed in the Law of Moses and rejected any other teaching or revelation. Angels and resurrection were things they didn't believe in. They believed in power, as many of the ruling families and priests were Sadducees.

In many ways, you can see glimpses of them in the way some Christians hold on to the past cling to the way things were or have always been. This behavior usually occurs when their power is threatened or perceived to be challenged. Try to get away with not wearing a suit or a tie in one of these churches or go to a meeting about the carpet color in the sanctuary! Fists and jaws get clenched in a hurry!

While many groups had a role in Jesus' death, the Sadducees had perhaps the most to lose if Jesus gained power. His teaching, healing, and claim to Kingship directly threatened all they held dear, not the least of which was the temple. Those losses were unacceptable, and they likely heaved a sigh of relief when Jesus was crucified.

The Law was the most critical part of Jewish identity. The Pharisees were the keepers of that Law. They were common people who accepted more than just Mosaic Law, including the Prophetic Books and wisdom literature. They loved the Law so much that, by the time of Jesus, they had identified over six hundred individual rules. It was vital for them to make sure everyone followed the Law because that is how they believed God's Kingdom would be established.

Similarly, bibliolatry is a common problem among Christians today. They read the Bible, but it goes further than that. The physical book itself takes on "mythical" proportions. These people take immense care with where their Bible is placed and how it's handled; some even refuse to get a new one. They get caught up in the book instead of practicing what it says. Further, Christians get keen on helping others follow the "rules," even when these people didn't sign up for that program. There is an expectation that folks who don't know Jesus, don't care, or don't understand should follow the rules anyway, and bibliolaters are happy to help them do it.

David says in Psalm 119:11, "I have hidden your word in my heart that I might not sin against you." Knowing *and* doing the Word is critical for a Christ-like engagement of our culture. Shaming others into living a Christian life is not the way.

Lastly, let's look at Zealots. In the first century, the Zealots were the ones who would fight to free Israel from her oppressors. Think of the Maccabean followers. Barabbas was likely a Zealot.

There aren't a whole lot of Christians running around advocating violence, but they are out there. They are the type who, in Jesus' name, kill doctors for performing abortions. To say this mentality doesn't make any sense would be putting it mildly.

This kind of thinking seeps into minds when the line between the nation and God gets blurred. Supporting the country is supporting God and vice versa. This is a very steep and scary path, and much harm has been done in the name of Jesus by people holding this perspective. Jesus didn't claim a nation, He claimed a Kingdom, and it wasn't gained by His violence, but by the violence done to Him.

Now, not everyone fits into these four categories, but they are fair generalizations about how people think and organize around a perceived need in today's world. From an explicitly Christian viewpoint, H. Richard Niebuhr's classic book *Christ and Culture* is a good examination of the directions we Christians tend to gravitate toward on a large scale.[5]

On a personal scale, we move in categories like Us vs. Them. We make things black and white so we can quickly identify where people fit and how they may behave. Putting people into binary categories makes it easy for us to determine who people are and where they stand. This applies to all areas of life.

"Oh, you are one of them."

"You vote like them."

"You think like them."

"You support what they support."

"You are not at all like me!"

When these conditions exist, they can become grounds for wholesale rejection of those we are called to love. Entire swathes of a culture can be lumped into a given category and summarily dismissed. I call this dynamic Othering.

The Others are everywhere. They lurk around every corner, in every mall, and in every restaurant and school. They serve you at theaters, teach your kids, take your money at the bank, and pour your coffee. Can you feel it? Can you sense the cold tingling down your spine when you think there are people out there who aren't like you? It's real, my friends, and if you aren't careful, they'll get you! They will change culture and laws, teach your kids the wrong things, infect society with their viruses, and kill the dreams of millions. They will challenge your worldview and communicate ideas you don't like. They will vote for people you won't vote for and push agendas you don't agree with. Simply put, they are out to ruin you.

This is how people felt about the Jews in Nazi Germany in the 1930s, and it's what helped turn a previously respected group of people into objects. Once people are objects, it doesn't take much for you to begin treating them as such. Ask the Rwandese what that produces. They will tell you what genocide looks like.

When people are The Other, they are "less than." They are no longer someone's child, mom, or dad. They are nothing. They have no feelings that count, no thoughts of value, no redeeming qualities or anything that could contribute to anyone. When that is the case, you can treat them any way you like. You can place them on rail cars like cattle—to begin with. And you know where this mentality leads.

> When people are The Other, they are "less than."

The truth is, we do this all the time. Maybe not literally, but in our minds. Every action begins as a seed in the mind, so those kinds of thoughts need to be challenged. Each human being has dignity. Every person on the planet deserves equal treatment, even when they disagree with you and even when they make you angry.

Think about what happens when you find out your friend, co-worker, or family member voted for Trump for President. Maybe you voted for Trump, and you've experienced people condemning you because of it. You may have ten thousand things in common with someone, but if they vote for the wrong candidate, they are out! Maybe you vote for abortion because you believe it is the woman's choice and you have experienced people calling you names. Perhaps you are gay, or you have gay friends, and the issues surrounding gay marriage produce conflict and Othering.

Honestly, you can pick any topic and there will be someone who disagrees and who will be happy to let you know you suck because you disagree with them. Men vs. women, dogs vs. cats, Ford vs. Chevy, Mac vs. PC—disagreement occurs all the time. These disputes are producing something in us as a society that didn't exist just a few decades ago. Forty or fifty years back, a disagreement didn't mean you hated someone; it meant you disagreed. Now, disagreement implies that you are full of hate, stupid, and not worthy of the skin you are outfitted with. The prevailing ethos is that if you disagree with someone, you hate them.

This hate, real or perceived, drives an incredible wedge between people when name-calling, culture-bashing, and Othering is the norm. It is normal to belittle. It is normal to attack. It is normal to make fun of those who don't agree with you. This isn't to our credit, and once we do these things long enough and with enough ferocity, we are only steps away from cattle cars.

It starts with your thinking. When we think of others as objects of hate, they cease to be people with meaningful relationships like us. They become The Other. *They are wholly different from us. They don't have the same dreams or hopes. They are our enemy, out to take what is ours. They are stupid.* You can clearly see this on the road. *That is why they drive slowly in the left lane.*

That's why they change lanes without using their blinkers. They are idiots because they don't drive like us. Driving is just a small example. There are any number of instances where our thinking is given over to the scary binary of Othering.

When that happens, this mentality quickly moves from our thoughts to our actions. One particular instance comes to mind.

My wife and I had the privilege of attending a conference in Hawaii. There aren't many places as breathtaking as those islands. We basked in the sun, enjoyed the gentle breezes, and had our fill of the ocean. We were like so many others who boarded the six-hour flight from Los Angeles, wanting to take in all the experience had to offer. People were so concerned with their vacations, though, that they failed to consider their fellow man.

We were in an ABC store to get some snacks one day. While walking down the aisle, I heard a sickening sound. You know, the kind of noise you hear that instantly tells you something is wrong? It was that sound. A hollow, slapping, skull-cracking sound.

I hurried to the end of the aisle to see what might have caused it. As I rounded the corner, I saw an elderly woman lying flat on her back in the middle of the checkout area. I ran to her side to see if she was okay. A pool of blood slowly began to form at the back of her head as it rested on the tile. I checked her pupils, held her hand, and encouraged her not to move.

Now, while this was happening, I noticed something else that was sickening. No one stopped to help. I had to interrupt someone to get an ambulance called. And, I kid you not, people literally stepped over her body to get to the tills. It was more important for them to continue their vacation than to try to help in some way.

I talked quietly with the injured woman and tried to reassure her she would be just fine. When the paramedics arrived, they took care of the gash on her head and loaded her onto a gurney and into the ambulance. I'm sure she recovered from her injuries, but I haven't recovered from mine. What does it take to step over a human being in such need?

She wasn't them. She didn't matter. They were on vacation. She was an object, like a LEGO, that should be stepped over. This is what happens when Othering moves from thinking to practice.

Another example. When I was a kid, I had a massive overbite. I'm not talking about a small one, but the kind that casts a shadow. My teeth arrived on the scene thirty seconds before I did. Now, I had the same wants, dreams, and desires as my classmates. I wanted to have friends. When we had recess, I wanted kids to play with, and I longed to be included in the football or kickball game. I wanted to belong.

But I was The Other. I was different. I looked different. I was an easy target for bullies and jokes. When you get treated like that, it doesn't take you long to begin to live into that role. I'm sure, in some ways, I did just that. That is the power of Othering. I believed what they said about me. My teeth were all people saw, and soon, they were all I saw. I wasn't a person; I was a beaver. I was a joke. I was a disease. As hard as it was, my brother's teeth were worse. We didn't have a lot of money. Joe was older and needed them worse, so he got braces first. It wasn't until I got braces that I had a small chance of seeing myself differently. But the damage was done. I was The Other, and I believed it.

When people become the problem, in whatever way, we introduce this dynamic. And it can get really scary really fast. People aren't problems to be solved; they are potentials to be realized. People are God's gift to us, to make us look more like Him. If they become problems to be solved, obstacles to step over, or diseases to avoid, we miss what God may want to accomplish in our encounter with them.

> **We can reinforce the God-given potential in every human being by our thoughts and actions.**

There are opportunities on personal and cultural levels to view people differently—better—if we choose to do so. *We can reinforce the God-given potential in every human being by our thoughts and actions.* We, as Christians, can create an environment where dignity is the norm and people receive shelter from all the biases of the world. I think that is what Jesus had in mind when He called us to love our neighbor: to love the world in the same way He did and provide a place for them to experience the grace and mercy we bask in every day.

Mark Twain wrote, "Everyone complains about the weather, but nobody does anything about it." I was struck by this comment like lightning. ☻ Wouldn't it be great if we could control the weather? As I write this, the United States is coping with massive devastation brought about by the weather. In the West, wildfires engulf parts of Oregon, California, Washington, Idaho, and my beloved Montana. Drought conditions and poor land management have produced charred lands on a level that hasn't been seen in over 100 years. If they had a little rain up there, the fires wouldn't be nearly as bad.

In Texas and the Gulf States, the last thing they need is a little rain! Large areas of Houston are under water from Hurricane Harvey. Hurricanes Irma and Jose are barreling down on the Caribbean and are threatening the East Coast. If we could somehow break up this force of nature, we could spare countless lives and save billions of dollars.

These events impacting the United States pale in comparison with the loss of life due to flooding in India, where 1,200 people recently lost their lives. If we could only control the weather, life would be easier. Right?

Of course, we would then argue about how much rain was needed, what the best temperature is, how much sun we can get, and on and on. Should it ever snow? Really, who likes to shovel snow?

Mark Twain was right—people complain, but nothing is done. Nothing can be done. Don't get me wrong, I believe the effects of global warming can be mitigated, but actually, can we control the weather? I don't think so. Could we achieve such god-like abilities in the future? It is possible, but for now, we are at Mother Nature's mercy.

It is not uncommon for people to feel powerless in the face of a thing like nature. We truly are powerless. We can experience that feeling when facing any number of things. An area of particular concern for Christians is our culture. Many believe that, at some point, the United States was a "Christian Nation." When we exhibit behavior unbecoming of such a nation, Christians want to reclaim our culture or keep it from spiraling into a perceived hellhole.

In her article in *Christianity Today*, Frederica Mathewes-Green points out that our culture is like the weather. "We may be able to influence it in modest ways, seeding the clouds, but it is a recipe for frustration to expect that we can direct it. Nor should we expect positive change without some simultaneous downturn in a different corner. Nor should we expect that any change will be permanent. The culture will always be shifting, and it will always be with us."[6]

In this brilliant piece, Frederica helps her readers see the role that Christians can play in cultural engagement. We have much to learn.

People try to control our culture by using money, influence, politics, shaming, name-calling, unfriending, and a whole host of other activities. Forgotten in all of this are the people who are "under the weather."

I live in the Phoenix area. For about five months of the year, it is like living near the gates of hell. It is hot. I can see Satan's shoes from here! But I grew up in Montana, and for about five months of the year, it is cold there. And grey. People need help with their sidewalks, getting snow shoveled and cars pushed out of snowbanks. Sometimes, they need a warm place to stay for a few moments before going out into the cold.

Everyone complains about the heat or the snow, but we can't change it. We can move if we don't like it, but the reality is, we all adapt and tolerate. In light of the weather here in Arizona, I believe our call is to provide shade and water. We are to be a place of rest for those who are suffering from what is happening in the skies above *and* on the ground. There are physical things we can do for those suffering from our actual climate and cultural climate, but there are also things we can do spiritually and emotionally. We can metaphorically shovel walks, give water, and provide shade.

My point is not that we should just give up on our culture. Far from it—I believe our acts can demonstrate an alternative lifestyle to the cultural norms. This, in turn, can and should speak volumes to our culture-shaping influences, including those people we put in office. However, the bulk of our time can't

> "We can't control the ocean, but we can learn to surf."

be spent figuring out ways to blot out the sun. It needs to be spent giving water to the thirsty. I heard this said once: *We can't control the ocean, but we can learn to surf.*

CHAPTER 5
WEATHER RESISTANT

Waterproof and breathable

The high school that my kids attend recently suffered another suicide. Despair seems to be rampant. People are worried, scared, addicted, lonely, shame-filled, financially strapped, and living moment to moment. All of this in an ever-increasingly polarized society that relies on one-liners on social media to deal with critical issues. This is helpful to no one. Especially those who are "under the weather."

Still, what is God doing? Why doesn't He do something? With all the horrors we see in our culture and around the globe—the violence, terrorism, and injustice—it begs the question: Does God care? This is one of the biggest issues people point to and say, "See, there is no God. If there is, He should do something!"

But God has done something.

Romans 12 is the pivotal chapter of Paul's letter to the Christians in Rome. Here, Paul turns from building his case for who God's people are to explaining life in light of all he has previously stated. Specifically, he calls Christ-followers to be living sacrifices. He calls us to be transformed, and as agents of transformation, to live with one another and the world in such a way as to represent Jesus to a needy world.

Paul frequently builds his case and then makes a summary statement. He does this in verses 9–21 of Chapter 12. He ends where I want to start with this statement: "Do not be overcome by evil, but overcome evil with good." What follows is how to do that very thing:

1. Let love be genuine. (Romans 12:9)

When our love is genuine—the kind of love that isn't only given to those who love us, love that doesn't come with strings attached or caveats—we overcome evil with good.

2. Abhor what is evil; hold fast to what is good. (Romans 12:9)

When we cease to practice evil and we despise it because we are holding so tightly to what is good, we overcome evil with good.

3. Love one another with brotherly affection. (Romans 12:10)

When we love one another with brotherly affection, we have no time or energy to point out and meditate on one another's flaws; we overcome evil with good.

4. Outdo one another in showing honor. (Romans 12:10)

When we make showing one another honor the point of our actions, we overcome evil with good.

5. Do not be slothful in zeal, be fervent in spirit, serve the Lord. (Romans 12:11)

When we make every effort to have a passionate response to Christ, we overcome evil with good.

6. Rejoice in hope, be patient in tribulation, be constant in prayer. (Romans 12:12)

When we are filled with hope, patience, and prayer, we overcome evil with good.

7. Contribute to the needs of the saints and seek to show hospitality. (Romans 12:13)

When we choose to use our resources in the service of others, we overcome evil with good.

8. Bless those who persecute you; bless and do not curse them. (Romans 12:14)

When we bless those who persecute us, we overcome evil with good.

9. Rejoice with those who rejoice, weep with those who weep. (Romans 12:15)

When we are with people in joy and sorrow, we overcome evil with good.

10. Live in harmony with one another. (Romans 12:16)

When we choose harmony rather than strife, we overcome evil with good.

11. Do not be haughty, but associate with the lowly. (Romans 12:16)

When we are humble and care for those less fortunate than us, we overcome evil with good.

12. Never be wise in your own sight. (Romans 12:16)

Humility overcomes evil with good.

13. Repay no one evil for evil, but give thought to do what is honorable in the sight of all. (Romans 12:17)

Choosing to end the cycle of sin and violence overcomes evil with good.

14. If possible, so far as it depends on you, live peaceably with all. (Romans 12:18)

Choosing to live at peace with those around you overcomes evil with good.

15. Beloved, never avenge yourselves, but leave it to the wrath of God, for it is written, "Vengeance is mine, I will repay, says the Lord." (Romans 12:19)

Trusting God with your pain overcomes evil with good.

16. To the contrary, "if your enemy is hungry, feed him; if he is thirsty, give him something to drink; for by so doing you will heap burning coals on his head." (Romans 12:20)

Loving your enemy overcomes evil with good.

17. Do not be overcome by evil, overcome evil with good. (Romans 12:21)

When Christians live this way, we give the world hope in the midst of hurricanes, earthquakes, fires, floods, crazy dictators, suicide, and all the other ills it faces. When people cry out "Why doesn't God do something?" they will have an answer because His people are so busy living out their faith. Jesus knows exactly what is needed. He knows the prescription for a broken world. It is you. It is Christ at work in you. *The Holy Spirit-infused work of God's people is His prescription for the ills of the world.* I can honestly tell you—practicing Romans 12:9–21 will overcome evil with good. It is the way to live in peace.

> The Holy Spirit-infused work of God's people is His prescription for the ills of the world.

Throughout much of my youth, I was bullied. I'm not talking about the kind of bullying that is sometimes annoying. I am talking about the kind that makes you dread going to school and hearing and feeling how unworthy you are. One particular student did nothing but wrong me, even to the point of assault.

After I gave my life to Christ, He began stripping away the shame and guilt I carried around. One of the ways He did this was by bringing to mind people I had wronged. Inevitably, as I prayed for forgiveness, they would reappear in my life. God graciously gave me opportunities to ask their forgiveness for how I had wronged them. It was cathartic and beautiful.

He also brought to mind the people who had wronged me. This was a different issue. I held on to my pain and bitterness toward those people. It felt good and right to do so. It took time, but I could eventually see how I was harming myself. In His typical fashion,

He reminded me of the anger I harbored toward my assailant. I wanted to be freed from what I willingly carried and prayed for forgiveness. Releasing those emotions and thoughts to Christ was amazing, but it wasn't enough. He had more work to do in me.

I needed to seek my bully's forgiveness for how I thought about and talked about him. I was thinking, "Are you kidding me, Jesus?" If I saw this guy again, I wanted to plow my fist into his face. I wanted nothing to do with him. But Christ won me over with His mercy. How could I ask others to forgive me when I wasn't willing to do the same?

One day, the bully walked into the store where I was working. I told God I wasn't ready. He said I was. I looked for others to help him. They were all busy. Reluctantly, I asked him if he needed help. In doing so, I found out he was leaving town; I would only get one shot at this forgiveness thing. As we walked to the counter, I took a deep breath and trusted Christ.

I turned to him mid-walk and said, "You know, I need to ask your forgiveness for all the bitterness I've held toward you all these years." Metaphorically, I closed my eyes and waited for the inevitable laugh or mockery. What happened next changed my life.

He extended his hand to me and said, "You are a lot further along in this Christianity thing than I am."

We shook hands, and he paid for his things and left. I haven't spoken to him since, but I am grateful for that moment every day I live. God was trying to do something *in* and *through* me. While I don't know how it will turn out, I know He wants to do the same with you.

Choose to be joyful. Feed someone you don't know. Listen to someone without giving advice. Spend time with someone you would usually not have time for. Remind people there is beauty in the world, beyond the Kardashians! Create something for someone. Write a note to someone using your own hand and a pen or pencil! Find ways to be kind to someone whom you find it hard to be kind to. Invite someone to join you under the umbrella you are using.

We are all "under the weather." The way out isn't to complain about it or try to stop the snow. It is to join one another *in* it and allow beauty and goodness to have a say.

I remember 9/11 like it was yesterday. I was getting ready for work and had the television on in the background. While I was getting ready to head out the door, I saw a plane had crashed into a building in New York City. CNN's red ticker tape slowly scrolled at the bottom of the screen, stating what had happened. A massive plume of smoke rose from the upper part of the tower. I remember thinking what a tragic accident it was. How could that happen? Equipment malfunction? Did the pilot have a stroke? It seems like it would be hard to crash a plane into a building like that.

Then the screen changed. It moved from the building to catch another plane on a similar course. I watched in horror and disbelief as it slammed mercilessly into the second tower. After a few fleeting moments, I realized people were doing this on purpose. Soon, reports came in about another plane. This plane was headed to the Pentagon. When it crashed, it took out a large section of the building, killing all on board and many on the ground. As waves of shock rolled over me, another plane was reported downed in Pennsylvania. It was like watching the unfolding of a horrifying new day, splattered with gasoline, fire, and blood.

My eyes were glued to the news. It only got worse. Shortly after the planes crashed into the buildings, they collapsed. The disintegration of the buildings killed thousands, either on the ground or in the buildings themselves. Over four hundred first responders died. The grayish white cloud of dust, paper, and debris covered the victims as they scattered for their lives. Story after story of people trying to help, first-person accounts, and others leaping to their deaths poured out of the television. Life would never be the same.

The impact of these events can be felt today. Anytime you go through an airport, you can see it. You have to take off your shoes because someone had an explosive device built into one of their sneakers. You are subject to searches or that weird machine that looks deep into your soul as it whirls around you and sends pictures of you without clothing somewhere across "The Network"! Armies of TSA agents greet you at various stages of your journey. It has all changed. Hopefully for the better.

We have been in the longest-running war in U.S. History. Afghanistan, home of Al Qaeda, has seen thousands of U.S. troops, munitions, planes, and other vehicles trace across her landscape to root out those responsible for the event. Over 27,000 combatants and over 30,000 civilians have lost their lives, the majority being Afghans themselves.

George W. Bush, in his speech to a joint session of Congress and the nation on September 20, 2001, said these words: "Our war on terror begins with Al Qaeda, but it does not end there. It will not end until every terrorist group of global reach has been found, stopped and defeated."[7]

Iraq was invaded in 2003 because it was believed they were stockpiling weapons of mass destruction. The occupation and invasion have cost thousands of lives and millions of dollars.

I could go on, but you get the drift. We are fighting terror, terrorists, and terrorism, foreign and domestic. When I heard Bush's speech, I remember thinking, "How can a bullet kill an idea? How can bombs stop terrorism? How won't this simply continue the cycle of violence and increase deep-seated hatred?"

Terrorists are The Other. They aren't people. They are things. They are uncivilized brutes who deserve what they get. Terrorists are filled with hate. Because they hate, we can hate them. Terrorists are violent. Because they are violent, we can be violent to them. As long as they are The Other, we can treat them any way we want.

I wish people understood better the complexity of American foreign policy. It would be helpful to see how our interactions with The Others were different in the not-so-distant past. But they don't. We don't. It is easier to spin a web of Othering, and it is easier for us to buy into that narrative.

It doesn't end with terrorists. Pick any group or person who doesn't think like you. Democrat, Republican, gay, straight, Christian, Muslim, black, white, pro-this, anti-that—it really doesn't matter. People fight one another over social and other issues in such a way as to cause Othering. Because they are the "enemy," you can think and do what you like with them. You can say what you believe and broadcast it to thousands with a simple tweet.

The particular social issue of the day is merely the stage where Othering takes place. In the words of a wise mentor of mine, Mel Sylvester, "How we do what we do is as important as what we do." This means that the *way* we make decisions, interact with one another, and talk about one another really matters. Having discussions without shouting, name-calling, or other dignity-smashing behaviors is critical if we hope to avoid the Othering pitfall. When we judge others, we take up the mantle Jesus has taken for Himself. He is the Judge. We are not. He judges fairly, and always with truth and love. We don't.

People aren't the problem. Fighting the Taliban, Al Qaeda, or any other terrorist group with bombs and guns won't fix the problem. There will always be terrorism, and if we fight this way, we will be in perpetual war. The apostle Paul knew this to be true. He knew and lived in the deep-seated hatred of first-century Judaism. Gentiles hated Jews, and Jews hated Gentiles. Jews hated Samaritans, and Samaritans hated Jews. But when he wrote to the Ephesians, Paul said this: "For our struggle is not against flesh and blood, but against the rulers, against the authorities, against the powers of this dark world and the spiritual forces of evil in the heavenly realms" (Ephesians 6:12). We can punch, kick, scream, and fight all we want, but it won't change the dynamic.

The reality is that many Christians have it all wrong.

The reality is that many Christians have it all wrong. We spend our energy in the wrong direction. We give money in the wrong places and pay attention to things that don't matter. I am one of them. It is easy to fall into these and other categories when striving to be like Christ and make an impact in this world. I give to aid organizations, support our troops, and seek to diminish the impact of terrorists here and abroad.

But I know there has to be a way forward that goes beyond any of those things. There has to be something that changes in them and me. Otherwise, we will increasingly move further away from one another and eventually destroy each other. Then only the strongest, meanest, most powerful, wealthiest, and most deceitful will survive. I don't want to live in that world. I bet you don't either.

CHAPTER 6

A LOVE OF ANOTHER KIND

*"They would change their tune, they would add
another measure, If they only knew this love
of another kind."*

—Amy Grant

Just as Jesus has taken on a myriad of different faces and functions, so too has love. Love has become the code word for any number of things. It can mean acceptance, forgiveness, always being kind, not being mean, tolerating someone, telling someone the truth, and a whole host of other activities. Like the idea of Jesus, these are all part of what Jesus was talking about when He mentions love, but they are not the full picture. This is especially true when it is used as a trump (not Donald) card for all arguments.

What did Jesus mean when He said "love the Lord your God," or "love your neighbor," or "love your enemy"? It is important to understand that there are different words for love in the original language of the New Testament. We will look at four. Each one has a different meaning, and some are used universally. So which ones did Jesus use, and why? Were they always the same word?

Before we answer these questions, let's first define love as best we can.

Love is complicated. It is an emotion, and it is an act of the will. It can be a verb and a noun. It touches everyone, but not everyone is in it. You can't always feel it, but you still know it's there. Love is weird. But love is important.

Merriam Webster describes love this way:

(1): strong affection for another arising out of kinship or personal ties, i.e., maternal love for a child

(2): attraction based on sexual desire: affection and tenderness felt by lovers; i.e., After all these years, they are still very much in love.

(3): affection based on admiration, benevolence, or common interests; i.e., love for his old schoolmates [8]

These definitions come from an ancient understanding of the nuances of love. Even thousands of years ago, love was a primary concern. The philosopher Plato is said to have written, "Every heart sings a song, incomplete until another heart whispers back. Those who wish to sing always find a song. At the touch of a lover, everyone becomes a poet."

Love can motivate us to our greatest heights and move us to our deepest despair. It is one of the most basic elements of being fully human. A life without love ceases to be life as it was intended. The apostle Paul called it the most excellent way.

> If I speak in the tongues of men or of angels, but do not have love, I am only a resounding gong or a clanging cymbal. If I have the gift of prophecy and can fathom all mysteries and all knowledge, and if I have a faith that can move mountains, but do not have love, I am nothing. If I give all I possess to the poor and give over my body to hardship that I may boast, but do not have love, I gain nothing.
>
> —1 Corinthians 13:1–3

Without love, you are a clanging cymbal or a resounding gong. You gain nothing and are, quite frankly, nothing. Those are strong words. If you give time to consider them, you can see the truth they carry. We are made for so much more than punching clocks, possessing wealth, and carrying on the species. Love is an integral piece of the human condition. The ancients knew it, and we know it.

Eros

Eros means sexual love or desire. Did Jesus want His followers to have sexual love or passion for God, neighbor, and enemy? Highly unlikely. However, it is essential to understand that there is nothing wrong with this type of love, and it is actually pretty important to the continuation of our species.

> "Not only does sex sell well, it wears well, it smells good, and it sleeps soundly."

In today's Western society, sex is everywhere. "Not only does sex sell well, it wears well, it smells good, and it sleeps soundly," according to the founder, designer, and CEO of Calvin Klein as quoted in Barbara Farfan's article in *The Balance*. [9]

According to Bradley Johnson, writing for *AdAge* in 2015, the top 200 national leading advertisers spent $137.8 billion in 2014.[10] That's $137.8 billion spent trying to figure out consumers: how they think, act, walk, talk, and make purchases, all so we can give them the money from our pockets.

It is as easy as the next Carl's Jr. advertisement. Eros has been twisted into something more than mere sexual feelings and procreative activity. It is leveraged for monetary gain. I know, I know—it has always been that way. How else would the world's oldest profession have gotten started? It seems people have always been willing to trade money for sex.

Movies like *50 Shades of Grey* (which made into the hundreds of millions according to Forbes[11]) illustrate how mainline the idea of eros has become. In fact, an *NBC News* business article states that "globally, porn is a $97 billion industry, according to Kassia Wosick, assistant professor of sociology at New Mexico State University. At present, between $10 billion and $12 billion of that comes from the United States."[12]

With that kind of leverage, it's no wonder that when people talk about love, they think sex. But love is more than sex. Love can encompass sex, but it certainly can't be replaced by it. Otherwise, you couldn't have love without sex, which you can—because I love hamburgers.

Confusing love and sex is common. The term "make love" is a euphemism for having sex. But you aren't making love. Sexual activity can be a result of the commitment to love, but you can have sex without love. (Unfortunately, that happens all of the time.) A friend once said of sex, "It's like a good dessert at the end of a great meal." The meal is the relationship, and sex is the outcome of the intimacy, trust, and love.

To be sure, sex is just a dessert; it isn't the whole meal. Even when people want to have dessert first, it is not enough to make a relationship work. If all you ate was dessert, you would become fat, sick, and really unattractive. Ice cream, cake, or whatever your choice of dessert may be only serves as the proverbial cherry on top. And love is so much more than that.

Having said all this, I'm pretty sure we aren't called to have eros for our neighbors and enemies. That would cause all sorts of problems and make Jesus blush. I would blush too. Really.

Phileo

Cities have their own flair and culture. Each one evokes memories, thoughts of historical events, musicians, and food. For example, Philadelphia is associated with the movie *Rocky*. *Rocky* symbolizes Philadelphia in a way that few things can. Tough, underdog, gritty—these words exemplify Philadelphia. Almost all Philadelphia sports teams and their fans show these traits. This gritty nerve also relates to the city's history—you certainly need those things if you are going to play a role in founding a nation.

Philadelphia was a center of rebellion and rebuilding as the colonies broke away from Britain and formed the United States. It even served as the U.S. capital for ten years.

And its cheesesteaks are amazing.

Why do I highlight Philadelphia? In case you didn't know, it is called the "city of brotherly love." The idea of brotherly love comes from the Greek word *phileo*, which is commonly used to talk about love in the Bible. There is a type of love you have for your brother, and unless this is a *Game of Thrones* reference (and it isn't!), it speaks of deep affection and a willingness to do whatever is needed for your "brother."

I have a brother named Joe. While we were in college, he had a disc removed from his back. The amount of pain he was in before surgery was incredible. When I went to see him in his room afterward, I was shocked at what I saw. He was standing in the middle of the room with his socks and hospital gown on, wearing his Walkman (kids, just think of a portable music device that only played music), and dancing! I freaked out, thinking he would fall in half or collapse at any moment. But he felt great! The pain was minimal compared to what he had experienced before.

Not long after that, the doctors gave him permission to start working out. We decided to play some basketball at the university in one of the recreation areas. Now, usually this wasn't a big deal and we had a pretty good time. This time, however, the people playing there were the kind of guys who thought they should be on a varsity team and wanted to save face in front of their fraternity brothers—so they competed like this was the Olympic Games.

Joe and I were not like those guys. Hoping to ease into things, we got onto a team and tried to have some fun. It didn't take long for that to end. One young man (who I will call Jonny) was really keen on winning and helping everyone understand how amazing he was. He decided to run my brother over at midcourt. Please understand—my view of violence has evolved over the years, but at that time, my primitive cerebral cortex was activated as I saw my post-op brother hit the floor.

I hurried down the court and stood over him with concern. Joe looked up at me and smiled. I asked, "Are you okay?"

For those of you who don't have brothers or aren't like the Sackett clan from Louis L'Amour, "Are you okay?" was code. It was code for:

> *Are you okay? Can you get up? Do I need to do anything? Would you like me to talk with Jonny? Would you like me to help Jonny not do that again? Would you like me to help Jonny not do that again through a variety of painful experiences? Want me to take Jonny out (not for coffee)? Want me to take out Jonny and his buddies? Want to join me?*

For Joe and me, that is what "Are you okay?" meant. And he knew it. With a smile, he said, "I'm good." I helped him up, and we slowly made our way off the court. Had my brother said otherwise, it would have been difficult to remember my faith. Jonny had no idea the Grim Reaper had been so close to paying him a visit.

That is part of brotherly love. And you can have this type of love for those who aren't your siblings. Take my friend Brian, for instance. Brian and I have been through much of life together. My kids call him "uncle," not because of biological reasons, but because there has to be some way of helping them understand the relationship he has with me, my wife, my parents, and, because of that, them.

We met in high school when neither of us knew who we were and what we were about. Both of us found different ways to seek identity on some level. We found a common thread in our ability to drink a lot of beer and have fun with a variety of people. But it wasn't like we had (or even have now!) much in common.

Brian is the consummate outdoorsman. He is an avid hunter, and he teaches agriculture education in Montana. He is a Gold Star Award winner as well as a Montana Outstanding Agricultural Education Teacher Award winner. The guy mountain bikes, and he even built a boat! Who does that! For a time, he did construction and was a contractor, so fixing things around the house or building items are no big thing for him.

On the other hand, I suck at fixing anything. I like the outdoors, but mainly when I'm with other people. Sports, books, history, and Brazilian Jiu Jitsu are more my things.

But it wasn't our hobbies that connected us. It was a common way of looking at life. We both determined that people and the way they interacted with life mattered. Brian had a way of putting things that helped me. Maybe it was because he was funny (he is a fantastic storyteller) or because he could be as irreverent as me, but we "got" each other. That's why we hung out.

After a night running around town, watching a movie, or some other venture, we would spend hours—and I mean hours—sitting in the car talking. Sometimes it was my driveway, sometimes his, but getting to either home was just a signal that the important stuff of life was about to start.

We wrestled with how we felt about family, friends, school, girls, and God. No topic was off-limits, and in the seat of Brian's car, I learned about my friend and myself. One time, after my family was dragged through the mud, Brian told me the truth about how I was handling it. "You are one bitter guy," he said. God, that stung. But he was right. And I desperately needed to hear it. That is what friends are for. He didn't know the impact that would have on me, and I am so grateful for his willingness to speak truth into my life.

We took legendary road trips to Missouri and Seattle, dodged elk, danced in clubs, fixed parking meters, escaped drug addicts, and laughed till our sides hurt.

We rededicated our lives to Christ around the same time. I remember desperately trying to figure out this Jesus thing, and going to a "Christian" concert seemed like a good idea to help. So, without shame, I admit that I went to see Amy Grant. The concert was during her "Baby, Baby" days, and I don't remember why, but Brian went with me. Among the screaming tweens and moms, the two of us stood out like sore thumbs. We were dancing (I *am* a far better dancer than Brian) and having fun when Amy Grant walked over to our area and waved at *me* (to this day, Brian gets this story wrong). *My walk with Jesus was complete.*

Somehow, someway, we got involved in Christian campus ministry at the University of Montana. Our faith grew, and because of that, so did our friendship. We met our wives during this time and had a ton of adventures. His path led him to agriculture and teaching, mine to history and seminary.

Life hasn't been all peaches and cream for Brian and his family, but they have an incredible spirit about them. His wife is fantastic and a good friend of mine, and his kids are a great reflection of them both: smart, funny, active, and loving. The Bays are beautiful people all the way around.

Do I love Brian? You bet. He is like a brother to me. Biological? Nope. But I know what it means to be loved, accepted, and challenged because of him. I know if I called, he would come running. That's brotherly love, and I am blessed to have both an incredible brother in Joe and an amazing brother in Brian.

Brotherly love doesn't have to be between guys. Obviously, you can have this type of relationship with sisters or anyone you consider to be family. Specifically, the bond between brothers is what the word is trying to get at. It's the perfect example of this phileo type of love.

I believe Jesus has this in mind when He calls us to love others. Is it the entire picture? No. But it is part of it. Having this kind of love for strangers, enemies, and neighbors is challenging. It is also life-changing. It changes them, us, and the rest of the world.

Storge

I have a confession to make. I don't know when it started, but I know I can't stop. It has been going on for so long that I don't want to stop it. It must have begun in my early adolescence, but I can't put my finger on a calendar and declare "Here is where it all began!"

It happens in public and at home. It happens when I'm alone and in front of guests. Some are incredibly offended by it. In fact, I have been told it isn't right and I need to stop, but it's a habit now. The horses are out of the barn, and there's no going back. It may soil my reputation, and you may look down upon me for admitting this, but here goes:

I call my mom by her first name.

Thanks for letting me get that off my chest. I feel a lot better now.

I know. I am a horrible person. For some, this practice is akin to sin. "How can you do that? Why do you do that? It isn't right! If my son called me by my first name … !"

It's weird for some, I know. The truth is, I won't let my teenagers call my wife or me by our first names (unless, of course, they start with Czar or Czarina, Divine Emperor, Most Magnanimous, or other lofty titles we have given ourselves).

So why do I call my mom by her first name and won't let my kids do it to me?

Because I'm a hypocrite, I guess.

Maybe you don't call your mom by her first name, but I bet your family does other things. I'll bet they are weird in some way like this too. I'll bet if you shared your family weirdness with me, I would squish up my face in utter disgust and confusion.

Like people who kiss their kids on the mouth. Weird! I think that is really gross. But for some families, it is entirely acceptable. This is the way they show affection, and it was probably passed down from their parents.

We don't do it, but you might. What about the family that's okay with publicly grooming one another like a troop of chimps, picking at one another's blemishes?

Or what about people who like that weird children's book, *I'll Love You Forever*, where the creepy mom won't let go of her kid and sneaks into his house? Aww, isn't that sweet?[13] No. No, it isn't. It's super weird. And if my mom did that, I would say, "Barb, get out of here! And when you do visit, use the door! Don't climb up the side of the house." Weirdo.

I am pretty judgmental, huh? I think you get the point, though. The kind of love that falls under these categories looks different for each of us. When preparing for work overseas, I was taught the phrase "It's not wrong, it's just different." Some of this family stuff falls into that box. *Storge*—familial love—is just like that.

> Love shared among family just looks different from the outside.

These are all ways in which people love one another. Families are weird. We all have our way of being together. It may not look like love to someone from the outside, but this is part of how clans communicate love—like a particular food made at a specific time of year or phone calls between a father and son over the results of a football game. *Love shared among family just looks different from the outside.*

One of the best ways my family shows love is by telling the truth. Honesty means a lot to us, and I know it doesn't work that way for everyone, but for us, it does. When my mom wanted to know how she looked in an outfit, she would ask *me*. Why? Because I would tell her the truth. "Do I look fat in this?"

"Yep."

"Ok, thanks."

Easy peasy. On the other hand, I know many families where that kind of communication would not be welcome. Those words would cause irreparable damage. The way you learn to give and receive love among family members is complicated. Many couches have been worn out in psychiatrists' offices because of these dynamics. But love is there. It may not be the way I would do it, but that doesn't mean it is any less important or influential.

This kind of familial love is usually reserved for those closest to us. But the call of Christ on our lives is to share even this with the rest of the world. It supposes a level of intimacy and trust. It's best not to walk around telling people "the truth in love" about looking fat. That doesn't translate well, and people generally don't receive that kind of love well. In fact, when Christians or others act like that, it is usually self-serving. The whole point of love is that it is other-centered.

Love can't be about meeting our needs. Even if someone looks fat, you don't share it with them—unless you have that kind of relationship. Even then, it's best to consider how it may be received at any particular time. Maybe try sharing your heart, life, and joys with someone for a while. See if love doesn't grow. Then, if they ask you if they look fat, you can pray about what to say!

Love of Another Kind: Agape

Love is for people we don't like and don't agree with.

This isn't a typical approach to love, I know. But this is what Jesus tells us.

> You have heard that it was said, "Love your neighbor and hate your enemy." But I tell you, love your enemies and pray for those who persecute you, that you may be children of your Father in heaven. He causes his sun to rise on the evil and the good and sends rain on the righteous and the unrighteous. If you love those who love you, what reward will you get? Are not even the tax collectors doing that? And if you greet only your own people, what are you doing more than others? Do not even pagans do that?
>
> —Matthew 5:43–47

Jesus wants love to govern all our relationships. On some level, it can be expressed through the various types of love we have discussed. But there is another love that captures Jesus' love best: *agape* love.

Agape love takes these other types of loves into account, but it goes a bit further. There is a beautiful nuance to agape. It says far more about the giver than it does the receiver. This kind of love points to where it originates as much as to how it functions or who benefits from it.

It is the kind of love expressed in 1 Corinthians 13. Before we look at that passage, I would like to get out my soapbox for just a moment. While this passage is used in countless weddings and people want to do creative things with it (like putting their names in the passage as a substitute for love, i.e., "Bob is patient, Bob is kind"), this passage talks primarily about how we are exercising our giftedness among one another. It isn't the mushy kind of love that gives you the "feels." It is a serious, volitional, intentional, focused practice. That kind of love does have a place in a wedding ceremony, and I think it is the most critical expression of love. So, as we look at it, I want to make sure we really know what we are examining. (Stepping down from box now, thank you.)

Agape is self-sacrificing. When we think about our interactions with those around us, it is easy to make people The Other, as previously explained. Without making objects out of people, agape love is Other-centered. This kind of love seeks the best for The Other. It isn't selfish. It doesn't assume it knows what's best for someone but seeks their good in every way. It asks, "What is the best way to love?" without assuming the answer.

Love is patient. What if we never lost patience with one another? Especially those we didn't like or agree with? What would the world think if Christians were as patient with others as God is with us?

Love is kind. It does not envy; it does not boast, it is not proud. If this statement about love is not the inverse of much of our cultural exchange, I don't know what is. Mean-spirited, envy-filled, swollen with pride—these kinds of interactions are the norm. Whether through the media, social media, internet, or elsewhere, fear drives our interactions. Like an injured dog, we bite and growl any time someone gets close to our pain. We lash out in fear that the pain will get worse, someone will know we are hurting, or we won't get what we need. But 1

John 4:18 says, "There is no fear in love. But perfect love drives out fear."

As Christians, we must bask in the love God has for us, and it will drive fear from our hearts. But if our primary orientation to the world is fear, it means some very significant things.

> As Christians, we must bask in the love God has for us, and it will drive fear from our hearts.

First, we aren't looking at things the way God does. John 3:16 tells us how God looks at the world: "For God so loved the world that he gave his one and only Son, that whoever believes in him shall not perish but have eternal life." God loves the world. I want to say that again, this time nice and loud. *GOD LOVES THE WORLD.* It isn't that He loved it at one time, sent Jesus, and then started hating it once He saw what they did with Him. He loves the world. Our orientation to the world is an expression of God's, filled with love. Compassion, grace, and mercy are the primary ways we have to show the world His love.

The second—and most terrifying—thing this means is that we are fearful because we think we are not being loved by God due to our sin. But we are His children. It is our right (and His pleasure) to crawl upon His lap, rest our head on His chest, and be loved. His love isn't based on our goodness. Romans 5:8 tells us that while we were still sinners, Christ died for us! So, He loves me regardless of my sin.

All that He has for me I can access at any time. Yes, even in the midst of my brokenness, I can come to Him. He is the fountain from which all our lives flow. He is the center of love we may have for the world. I have to receive from Him in order to give. We love because He first loved us! If we as God's children are not experiencing what the Father has for us, how in His name will the world experience His love? Christians are called to be the conduit through which God's love flows to the world. If the world is scary or unlovely, we can look to Him. We can also wonder if we are doing our job or not.

Imagine calling the fire department to come put out a fire. If they show up and decide they are too afraid to fight it, where is the hope? If Christians are doing their job—being loved by God, loving God, and loving their neighbor, including their enemy—those who are fearful have a place to turn. The world will have hope.

It does not dishonor others; it is not self-seeking, it is not easily angered, it keeps no record of wrongs. When the church co-opts the world's view on how to interact with one another, we lose our voice. We are no different from the world in our behaviors, ideas, and practices. Why should anyone listen to us? If people who are called to love always dishonor others, keep only their own interests, get angry, and have a long record of how they have been wronged, no one will join them. And no one should.

Unfortunately, this is how much of the church has responded to the world. Instead of forgiving, honoring, and peace-seeking, we have driven wedges between people and opted for playing the role of Judgmental Jesus. When we choose this, we are no better than anyone else.

Love never fails. There is a reason Jesus chose to love. It works. Paul says it never fails. Love works on us and The Other. When we decide that love is the way forward, we take the sword out of the hand of our attackers. They may inflict damage or even kill, but a life of loving an enemy resonates most deeply over time.

Someone recently pointed out that the "love thing" got Jesus killed. "Look what they did to Him." I responded, "Look what He did for us." Even from the cross, Jesus asked His Father to forgive His killers. Two thousand years later, we are still talking about it. Why? Because love works. Our determination to love keeps us from bitterness, anger, unforgiveness, pride, and any number of other diseases. Our lives are better when we choose to love.

In one of my favorite quotes, Thomas Merton says, "Our job is to love others without stopping to inquire whether or not they are worthy. That is not our business, and, in fact, it is nobody's business. What we are asked to do is to love, and this love itself will render both ourselves and our neighbors worthy."[14]

May it be so.

The Four Loves by C.S. Lewis is a far more nuanced look at love than I have written.[15] He does a fantastic job of looking at it from the four angles of eros, phileo, storge, and agape, but he adds much more. Particularly, he shows how the different loves interact in various ways. I can't recommend reading it enough. That guy is pretty smart.

Luke also records an important interaction on this point in Chapter 10 of his Gospel.

> On one occasion an expert in the law stood up to test Jesus. "Teacher," he asked, "what must I do to inherit eternal life?"
>
> "What is written in the Law?" he replied. "How do you read it?"

He answered, " 'Love the Lord your God with all your heart and with all your soul and with all your strength and with all your mind'; and, 'Love your neighbor as yourself.' "

"You have answered correctly," Jesus replied. "Do this, and you will live."

But he wanted to justify himself, so he asked Jesus, "And who is my neighbor?"

In reply, Jesus said: "A man was going down from Jerusalem to Jericho when he was attacked by robbers. They stripped him of his clothes, beat him and went away, leaving him half dead. A priest happened to be going down the same road, and when he saw the man, he passed by on the other side. So too, a Levite, when he came to the place and saw him, passed by on the other side. But a Samaritan, as he traveled, came where the man was; and when he saw him, he took pity on him. He went to him and bandaged his wounds, pouring on oil and wine. Then he put the man on his own donkey, brought him to an inn and took care of him. The next day he took out two denarii and gave them to the innkeeper. 'Look after him,' he said, 'and when I return, I will reimburse you for any extra expense you may have.'

"Which of these three do you think was a neighbor to the man who fell into the hands of robbers?"

The expert in the law replied, "The one who had mercy on him."

Jesus told him, "Go and do likewise."

In many ways, we are like the expert in the Law. We try to find a way around what we are told. Luke says he was trying to justify himself. "And who is my neighbor?" is a way of trying to sort out who we are supposed to love. Jesus brought it home rather quickly. A Samaritan was a better neighbor than the priest and the Levite.

It could be expected that priests and Levites would be the ones to show mercy to the traveler, but they didn't. They were God's people, chosen to represent Him to the world. They had prominent positions leading the people in worship. But, for whatever reason, they didn't act.

Pulling the parable apart a bit, we can see some "justifiable" reasons for them not to. Touching someone in the state Jesus describes, beaten and half-dead, would mean real problems. They might come in contact with blood. This would make them ceremonially unclean. If they were unclean, they would have trouble performing their God-given duties. God wouldn't want that, would He? In fact, they passed by "on the other side" so as to avoid even the appearance of being unclean. "What would people say if they saw me dealing with this person?" If he was dead, they couldn't come in contact with him either. So dead, alive, or somewhere in between, they didn't act.

Some may say that the person deserved what happened. It is foolish to take the road from Jerusalem to Jericho alone. It is a dangerous road and known for robbers and peril. What did you think would happen? Because you did something so stupid, you deserve it, and I'm not going to help you. But weren't the priest and the Levite traveling alone as well?

A Samaritan was the one whose actions Jesus condones, yet Samaritans were enemies to the Jews. They were a "mixed" race of Jews who worshiped at a different temple. Jews hated Samaritans and vice versa. But this one decides to act. Nothing he does is convenient. He stops his journey, which could put doubt in the mind of his loved ones about his own safety. ("Shouldn't he have arrived by now?") He cared for the man's wounds, exposing himself to the whole "unclean" thing. He put the man on his donkey. This meant he himself had to walk. Jericho is roughly sixteen miles from Jerusalem, so wherever it happened, the Samaritan traveled a long way. He exposed himself to further danger. A man walking a donkey with a nearly dead man on it would be an easy target. As if that weren't enough, he spends his money on this guy as well. He pays for his stay at the inn, *and* he is willing to take care of further expenses when he comes by the next time. Talk about going the extra mile!

The entire passage is kicked off by a question that was a typical litmus test for righteousness at the time: "What must I do to inherit eternal life?" Jesus uses the opportunity to help reshape the discussion. It isn't just about eternal life; it is about how we are the people of God and what that means here and now. The keeper of the Law wanted a quick answer, one that would place Jesus in one camp or another. He wasn't looking for *how* we should treat one another but *who* we should treat with love.

Similar to the Law keeper, we don't ask the question about our neighbor but about love. Loving your neighbor or enemy is all well and good, but what *kind* of love are you talking about? This is precisely why I wrote about it. It's easy for us to parse words in our minds, to work around things we find too difficult or even impossible for us.

And still, this is what Jesus calls us to do.

Love looks like some beautiful cocktail of all four loves. Of course, eros would be reserved for particular relationships, but if you look at phileo, storge, and agape, you get a clearer picture of what Jesus was talking about. Love looks like all those. Love looks like being the type of person who is willing to share this kind of love with those around them, regardless of their worth.

To put it practically, Jesus calls us to become "unclean" when it comes to loving others. Our neighbor is the one in need. It doesn't matter who they are or why they are there. We are to love them, not in the way our culture says to, but in the way Jesus says to. That means ceremonial uncleanliness, socially questionable practices, and a willingness to care for others that supersedes our own convenience. It means loving The Other: the black, white, red, yellow, brown, mixed, gay, straight, transgendered, Democrat, Republican, flag-waving, protesting, Christian, Muslim, Buddhist, atheist, immigrant (legal or otherwise), refugee, poor, wealthy, privileged, disadvantaged, challenged, older, younger, self-entitled, mean-spirited, hate-filled, bigoted, sexist, and wounded. Did I miss anyone?

Yeah, them too.

CONCLUSION

At the beginning of the book, we found out that Ricky Bobby likes the baby version of Jesus the best. Cal likes to picture Jesus in a tuxedo T-shirt, with eagle's wings, singing lead for Lynyrd Skynyrd with an angel band, ready to party at the drop of a hat. Walker likes to picture a ninja Jesus fighting off evil samurai. Everyone has a favorite way to portray Jesus. Hopefully, you have examined your relationship with Him and called into question your own preferences. And if you have a Twitter account, you haven't tweeted #NotMyJesus!

Jesus is more than what we like to think about Him. If we insist on our way of viewing Jesus, our one way of thinking about Him, we miss what God was doing in and through Him. He didn't come to make us feel better. He came because of our deep need. And when God, who knows all about us, decides what we need, we don't get to tell Him otherwise or that we only want it a certain way. Like petulant children, we only take the medicine we like or that tastes good. If we continue this way, we don't get better.

Beyond this, we may be contagious, spreading our preconceived and well-loved ideas about Jesus with a negative effect. One look at our culture will tell you this has occurred. Incomplete pictures of Jesus don't just dot the landscape, they are dominant features. People walk away from the faith because their version of Jesus didn't work, despite the fact that it may have been an incomplete or, heaven forbid, inaccurate understanding of who He is and what He was about.

Jesus refused any one category that didn't have to do with His vocation. This is why He was such a provocative figure. People couldn't put Him into the roles they wanted Him to fill. When He didn't look like the King or Messiah that the people wanted, they turned on Him.

Think about what happened with Barabbas. Releasing Barabbas instead of Jesus reveals the depths of despair and disappointment those gathered in Jerusalem must have felt. How could you want a notorious criminal freed (he didn't just steal a piece of candy) instead of the man who healed the sick and diseased?

Jesus was doing so much more than creating a political movement or challenging Rome. He did those things, just not in the way you would imagine. Jesus knew the real problem lay within the hearts of men, women, children, and eunuchs. And the only way to deal with that was to function as Israel's true Messiah. This didn't mean a short-lived revolt or the establishment of a king who ruled like all other kings. Jesus said in John 14:6, "I am the way and the truth and the life. No one comes to the Father except through me."

His life wasn't about simple ideas of ruling, kingship, power, or even platitudes about how God worked. He claimed a unique position for Himself, and nothing deterred Him from that vision. He would free God's people from her oppressors in a way they

He was taking on sin, hell, and death. And He won.

could never imagine. It wasn't enough to defang Rome and the religious leaders; *He was taking on sin, hell, and death. And He won.*

This vocation gives Jesus every right to be judgmental. John says of Jesus in Revelation 19:11, "And I saw heaven opened, and behold, a white horse, and He who sat on it is called Faithful and True, and in righteousness, He judges and wages war." Further on, in Chapter 22, Jesus says, "I am the Alpha and the Omega, the First and the Last, the Beginning and the End." And Paul says in Colossians 1,

> For he has rescued us from the dominion of darkness and brought us into the kingdom of the Son he loves, in whom we have redemption, the forgiveness of sins.

> The Son is the image of the invisible God, the firstborn over all creation. For in him all things were created: things in heaven and on earth, visible and invisible, whether thrones or powers or rulers or authorities; all things have been created through him and for him. He is before all things, and in him, all things hold together. And he is the head of the body, the church; he is the beginning and the firstborn from among the dead so that in everything he might have the supremacy. For God

> was pleased to have all his fullness dwell in him, and through him to reconcile to himself all things, whether things on earth or things in heaven, by making peace through his blood, shed on the cross.

The Guy who has accomplished all these things and bears these truths in His very person surely has the right to judge you and me. I can't even make dirt. Can you? We are freed to live the lives He calls us to live. We don't have to hide; we don't have to worry or have shame because He knows it all. We know He knows. He calls it like it is, and when He does, we can turn to the same Guy who so freely offers the grace and mercy we need. It is a pretty fantastic thing to have the judge pay your fine.

Jesus told a story illustrating this—but with a warning—as seen in Matthew, Chapter 18:

> Then Peter came to Jesus and asked, "Lord, how many times shall I forgive my brother or sister who sins against me? Up to seven times?" Jesus answered, "I tell you, not seven times, but seventy-seven times. "Therefore, the kingdom of heaven is like a king who wanted to settle accounts with his servants. As he began the settlement, a man who owed him ten thousand bags of gold was brought to him. Since he was not able to pay, the master ordered that he and his wife and his children and all that he had be sold to repay the debt. At this, the servant fell on his knees before him. 'Be patient with me,' he begged, 'and I will pay back everything.' The servant's master took pity on him, canceled the debt and let him go."

This is precisely what Jesus has done for us, and what He wants us to do for others.

> "But when that servant went out, he found one of his fellow servants who owed him a hundred silver coins. He grabbed him and began to choke him. 'Pay back what you owe me!' he demanded. His fellow servant fell to his knees and begged him, 'Be patient with me, and I will pay it back.'"

Notice how this fellow servant uses the same words the wicked servant used to his master.

> "But he refused. Instead, he went off and had the man thrown into prison until he could pay the debt. When the other servants saw what had happened, they were outraged and went and told their master everything that had happened. Then the master called the servant in. 'You wicked servant,' he said, 'I canceled all that debt of yours because you begged me to. Shouldn't you have had mercy on your fellow servant just as I had on you?' In anger his master handed him over to the jailers to be tortured until he should pay back all he owed. This is how my heavenly Father will treat each of you unless you forgive your brother or sister from your heart."

Jesus is Judge, but He will also pay our fine. In return, He expects us to be forgiving. He expects us to live like we are loved and have mercy on those around us. But we often get it twisted. We wind up trying to take on the role Jesus has reserved for Himself.

Jesus is the Judge. We are not. When we get our roles reversed, we cause all manner of problems. People "under the weather" are uncared for by the very people who are called to care for them, and we take the position reserved for the Son of God. It isn't unlike the story told through the nation of Israel.

The Jews were God's people, a mantle they proudly wore. They told stories about how God acted on their behalf by rescuing them in different situations or providing for them miraculously. However, the point was that they would be a beacon, a giant neon sign flashing in the darkness that says "Find God here!" The way they lived was supposed to point to the God who saves, a light even to the Gentiles. But it didn't work that way. Instead, they fell in love with the Law they were given and worried more about how to follow it than what the purpose was for the Law.

North American Christians are similar. Many are more worried about what they are saved from, not what they were saved to and to do! The identity, purpose, and passion of God's people are lost among the myriad efforts Christians make to stay relevant or defend the Bible. To do so, they become bibliolaters: worshippers of the Bible, not of the One it reveals.

> **When the purpose behind the work of God is lost on His people, their hearts become hardened and fearful.**

When the purpose behind the work of God is lost on His people, their hearts become hardened and fearful. Instead of trying to reach those in great need of care, they amplify divisions and create false dichotomies. The Other arises and Christ's role is reversed, making it His job to love and ours to judge. When that happens, everyone loses.

Christians don't fulfill God's call on their lives, and The Other remains an object. Our job—to love God, our enemies, and our neighbors—remains undone.

So what do we do with this role-reversal dilemma?

The God of the universe has decided what prescription the world needs. If He loved the world, then the prescription for the world's ills isn't more judgment, division, Othering, or bombs. Somehow, some way, the answer is love. But when God's people are more preoccupied with being right than being beautiful, the answer remains hidden. If Christians operate their lives out of fear instead of faith, the world will continue to suffer.

Remember, 1 John 4:18 says, "There is no fear in love. But perfect love drives out fear." We must learn to be loved by God. We must do a better job of basking in His grace and mercy for us. Then we can turn our attention to those around us. You can't give away what you don't have. Operating from a place of fear creates more fear and worry. The world doesn't need more of that. It has plenty of its own.

We must love with reckless abandon. Wouldn't the world look different if Christians practiced what they said they believed? I don't mean culturally or politically. I mean, what if—as the world has its way with people and isolation increases and divisions deepen—people had a place to turn? The church would be a place of safety and refuge for those harassed souls looking for hope. I believe, along with Bill Hybels, that the local church is the hope of the world. Its influence would only increase if we learned to receive God's love and, in turn, give it away. We might actually look like the Guy we say we follow. Not a caricature of Him, not a picture through a keyhole, but the full image of Christ in all His judgmental goodness. People flocked to Jesus for a reason. Is it too much to think that God's people, empowered by His Holy Spirit, might be attractive to a world in need?

Jesus' intention for His people was to make sure that love governed every human interaction. That is why He included enemies (not wives, husbands, children, or relatives, but enemies) in the call for love. He'll take care of anything else. Our job is to love. Clinging like a drowning rat to an incomplete picture of Jesus makes it next to impossible to live out this mission.

> **Love is His idea, and He is actually pretty smart.**

If Jesus isn't Judge, if He isn't Messiah, then we don't know who is in charge. We think someone needs to be the judge, so we step up to the plate. But He is those things, and we can trust Him. *Love is His idea, and He is actually pretty smart.*

Maybe we should follow Him and see what happens. We are invited into the beautiful, mystical, powerful work of God in and through Jesus Christ. Empowered by His Holy Spirit, we have the opportunity to change the world!

We don't have to judge or fight against people, or the culture, or evil samurai. Instead, we will fight against our desire to be selfish. We will fight against fear in every area of our lives and demonstrate to a scared, fear-filled world that there is a God who loves them deeply, and because of His work, so do His people.

May it be ever so. #MyJesus

LOVE QUOTES

Martin Luther King Jr.

"Darkness cannot drive out darkness: only light can do that. Hate cannot drive out hate: only love can do that."
—*A Testament of Hope:*
The Essential Writings and Speeches

"Love is the only force capable of transforming an enemy into a friend."
—*Strength to Love*

"I have decided to stick with love. Hate is too great a burden to bear."
—*Where Do We Go from Here?*

"Man must evolve for all human conflict a method which rejects revenge, aggression, and retaliation. The foundation of such a method is love."

—Acceptance Speech, Nobel Peace Prize

Thomas Merton

"Love is our true destiny. We do not find the meaning of life by ourselves alone—we find it with another."

—*Love and Living*

"The beginning of love is to let those we love be perfectly themselves, and not to twist them to fit our own image. Otherwise, we love only the reflection of ourselves we find in them."

—*No Man is an Island*

"Love seeks one thing only: the good of the one loved. It leaves all the other secondary effects to take care of themselves. Love, therefore, is its own reward."

—*No Man Is an Island*

"Our job is to love others without stopping to inquire whether or not they are worthy. That is not our business, and in fact, it is nobody's business. What we are asked to do is to love, and this love itself will render both ourselves and our neighbors worthy."

—*Disputed Questions*

Brennan Manning

"My deepest awareness of myself is that I am deeply loved by Jesus Christ, and I have done nothing to earn it or deserve it."

—The Ragamuffin Gospel

"Define yourself radically as one beloved by God. This is the true self. Every other identity is illusion."

*—Abba's Child: The Cry of the Heart
for Intimate Belonging*

C.S. Lewis

"This is one of the miracles of love: It gives a power of seeing through its own enchantments and yet not being disenchanted."

—A Grief Observed

"To love at all is to be vulnerable. Love anything, and your heart will be wrung and possibly broken. If you want to make sure of keeping it intact you must give it to no one, not even an animal. Wrap it carefully round with hobbies and little luxuries; avoid all entanglements. Lock it up safe in the casket or coffin of your selfishness. But in that casket, safe, dark, motionless, airless, it will change. It will not be broken; it will become unbreakable, impenetrable, irredeemable. To love is to be vulnerable."

—The Four Loves

"Love is not affectionate feeling, but a steady wish for the loved person's ultimate good as far as it can be obtained."

—*God in the Dock*

Others

"Love is of all passions the strongest, for it attacks simultaneously the head, the heart, and the senses."

—Lao Tzu, Chinese Philosopher

"Logic cannot comprehend love; so much the worse for logic."

—N.T. Wright, *Surprised by Hope: Rethinking Heaven, the Resurrection, and the Mission of the Church*

"The world is indeed full of peril, and in it, there are many dark places; but still there is much that is fair, and though in all lands love is now mingled with grief, it grows perhaps the greater."

—J.R.R. Tolkien, *The Fellowship of the Ring*

"You don't love because: you love despite; not for the virtues, but despite the faults."

—William Faulkner, *Mississippi*

"No one is born hating another person because of the color of his skin, or his background, or his religion. People must learn to hate, and if they can learn to hate, they can be taught to love, for love comes more naturally to the human heart than its opposite."

—Nelson Mandela, *Long Walk to Freedom*

"It takes courage to love, but pain through love is the purifying fire which those who love generously know. We all know people who are so much afraid of pain that they shut themselves up like clams in a shell and, giving out nothing, receive nothing and therefore shrink until life is a mere living death."
—Eleanor Roosevelt, *My Day: The Best Of Eleanor Roosevelt's Acclaimed Newspaper Columns, 1936-1962*

"Keep love in your heart. A life without it is like a sunless garden when the flowers are dead."
—Oscar Wilde, *In Conversation*

"If you would be loved, love, and be loveable."
—Benjamin Franklin, *Poor Richards Almanac*

"To love means loving the unlovable. To forgive means pardoning the unpardonable. Faith means believing the unbelievable. Hope means hoping when everything seems hopeless."
—G.K. Chesterton, English Author and Apologist

"When I despair, I remember that all through history the way of truth and love have always won. There have been tyrants and murderers, and for a time, they can seem invincible, but in the end, they always fall. Think of it—always."
—Mahatma Gandhi

"Love is patient, love is kind. It does not envy, it does not boast, it is not proud. It is not rude, it is not self-seeking, it is not easily angered, it keeps no record of wrongs. Love does not delight in evil but rejoices with the truth.

It always protects, always trusts, always hopes, always perseveres."

—The Apostle Paul

"Perhaps all the dragons in our lives are princesses who are only waiting to see us act, just once, with beauty and courage. Perhaps everything that frightens us is, in its deepest essence, something helpless that wants our love."

—Rainer Maria Rilke, *Letters to a Young Poet*

"Love is for people we don't agree with and people we don't like."

—Bob Fabey

ACKNOWLEDGMENTS

When God put me together, He knew how much I would need encouragement and kindness. My wife, Amy, does that and so much more. She is incredible on every level. I can't be who I am without her. Her patience and witness for Christ is beautiful.

J.P. and Hannah are PKs (pastor's kids). They have handled this with grace and dignity. I couldn't be prouder of who they are and who they are becoming. They love, serve, lead, and are wise beyond their years. I couldn't possibly love you guys more.

Mom and Dad—Thanks for being the "wedge breakers." Your courage to follow Christ demonstrates this statement beautifully: "It ain't how you start, it's how you finish." Thanks for making a point of living and finishing well.

Joe—I am so proud to be your brother. Your character and bravery encourage me. You have a huge heart and a sharp mind, and although I am bigger, stronger, more handsome, and funnier, you will always be my big brother.

Roen clan. Thanks for welcoming me with open arms. I love you guys.

Brian and the Bays—I said enough about you in the book. You are the best. Thanks.

To everyone at Music Serving the Word Ministries—it is a joy to work with you and to creatively share the love of Jesus with those around us. Thank you.

Living Faith Anglican Church and the greater Anglican world—Thanks for allowing me to serve you and for helping bring healing and true community to our family.

To all my CMA friends—I am so grateful for my formation in the Christian and Missionary Alliance and for Christ's heart that you so clearly display.

Tony Cummins, Mabiala Kenzo, Rod Remin, Ray Downey, Mel Sylvester, George Durance and many others at Canadian Theological Seminary (now Ambrose University)—Thanks for your patience with this theologically sensitive "redneck" as I tried to sort through the depths of my MDiv. You continue to make a significant impact on my life. To my classmates at CTS, many of whom I am still in touch with, thanks for continuing to encourage me in my walk with Jesus. Although it has been over 20 years, I would like to thank the people of Missoula Alliance Church. You provided a place for me and Amy to grow, become baptized, and get married. Especially thanks to Jeff Valentine.

To my CRU peeps—I owe so much of who I am to you. Whether on the U of M campus, in Tahoe, or in Kyrgyzstan, you have changed me forever.

To my teachers at Big Sky and around Missoula—Thanks for not killing me. You helped me believe in myself. Thanks, Mr. Jones, for the time you made me make a list of the good things about me and the bad. Although it took years to sink in, your belief in me and that moment has made a huge difference. Bob Womack, even though you like the Bobcats, I think I owe much of my love for history to you. "Rawhide!" "5 pages."

I know I am missing so many of you. Please forgive any oversight. Maybe I will publish a book of nothing but names.

Finally. Jesus has been willing to take this dirt, add some water, and mold me lovingly. The acceptance, joy, peace, and mercy I find in Him is beyond description. I know I doubt and wrestle. I know I fail. But if I can in some way, somehow, give people around me a picture of what He is like, that's enough. Thanks for loving me and letting me love You.

ENDNOTES

1 McKay, Adam, et al. *Talladega Nights: the Ballad of Ricky Bobby.* Sony Pictures Entertainment, 2006.

2 Musker, John and Ron Clements, directors. *Aladdin.* Walt Disney, 1992.

3 http://godhatesfags.com/

4 Wright, Nicholas Thomas. *The New Testament and the People of God.* SPCK, 2002.

5 Niebuhr, H. Richard. *Christ and Culture.* Harper & Row, 1975.

6 http://www.christianitytoday.com/ct/2006/ march/10.36.html

7 https://georgewbush-whitehouse.archives.gov/news/ releases/2001/09/20010920-8.html

8   "love." *Merriam-Webster.com*. 2017. https://www.merriam-webster.com (9 September 2017).

9   https://www.thebalance.com/calvin-klein-quotes-about-marketing-sexuality-2892507

10   http://adage.com/article/advertising/big-spenders-facts-stats-top-200-u-s-advertisers/299270/

11   https://www.forbes.com/sites/scottmendelson/2017/02/12/box-office-fifty-shades-darker-whips-up-146m-worldwide-debut/#55db6a6e93d5

12   http://www.nbcnews.com/business/business-news/things-are-looking-americas-porn-industry-n289431

13   Munsch, Robert N., and Sheila ill. McGraw. *Love You Forever*. Firefly Books, 1986.

14   Merton, Thomas. *Disputed Questions*. Harcourt Brace Jovanovich, 1985.

15   Lewis, C. S. *The Four Loves*. HarperOne, 2017.

84028906R00082

Made in the USA
San Bernardino, CA
02 August 2018